The Teacher and
Collective Bargaining

THE PROFESSIONAL EDUCATION SERIES

The Teacher and Collective Bargaining

by

ROBERT L. WALTER

Professor of
Educational Administration
Temple University

PROFESSIONAL EDUCATORS PUBLICATIONS, INC.
LINCOLN, NEBRASKA

Library of Congress Catalog Card No.: 74-16835

ISBN   0-88224-094-3

Contents

Introduction

The process of collective negotiations has propelled American teachers into new relationships, with new opportunities and new problems. This has all happened rapidly. Many teachers with years of experience have found that severe changes have come about. Those just beginning to teach find that complexities and necessary decisions crowd upon them, many stemming from this new circumstance.

Opportunities abound! Teachers in many communities have a guaranteed role founded in legislation which requires that employing boards of education meet with their representatives on an equal basis to decide matters of critical importance to teachers. Collectively teachers can exert power far beyond what many dared imagine only a few years ago.

Collective bargaining is played out by representative organizations operating under laws and precedents that stylize behavior. The teachers who are being represented need to understand these ground rules if they are to judge the quality of the representation afforded them. The representative organizations need understanding from their members if they are to mount effective bargaining efforts on their behalf.

Problems exist for teachers and for boards of education. Collective bargaining is a process developed in an industrial setting in response to the social and economic conditions of the first third of this century. Whether that mechanism is well designed for use in public employment in the last third of the century is open to some debate. Teacher organizations have successfully pushed for negotiations laws in many states. Most teachers in this country are now employed in systems where their conditions of employment are determined through collective negotiations. Yet difficult questions pertaining to the implementation of the process remain unsettled.

Teachers are not the only ones affected by the onset of collective negotiations. Parents and other concerned citizens, who hold the final power in public education, also need to understand something of this process. The effect of negotiations on the management of schools, on

7

the supervision of instruction, on the allocation of available funds, and on the way decisions affecting their children are made are all legitimate matters of concern to them.

Much information about negotiations comes from partisan sources. Teachers' organizations and boards of education are in an adversary relationship. Teachers are told about negotiations by their organizations. Such explanations inevitably reflect the advocacy status legitimately held by these organizations. Citizens may be briefed by school-board members and state school-board associations. Their presentations also reflect the tensions of the adversary relationship.

This book is designed as a primer for all: teachers, parents, school-board members, administrators, and interested citizens. It is written in the belief that collective negotiation is essentially a conservative force in public education; conservative in that it is designed to work within the existing democratic system. The author has worked intimately with both parties to collective bargaining. That experience has led to a conviction that most boards of education and most teacher organizations are, in the long run, committed to the same end. Both seek to develop the capacity of school districts to deliver educational services to pupils in an effective way. This is not to suggest that bitter differences do not exist in many communities about how this is to be accomplished, or even about defining good educational services. But collective bargaining provides a means by which bitter differences can be accommodated, with both sides accepting a basic common purpose.

A primer is written for those who are just beginning to learn. Many readers will have had some contact with unionism and collective bargaining within and without public education. This book is offered in the hope that a discussion of the process and of some problems and issues connected with it will help teachers and parents alike better to understand the forces that bear upon them and the opportunities each have to deal with these forces effectively.

A bibliography is appended because much of importance remains unsaid in this book. Those who accept leadership positions in teacher organizations or in the administration of public education should undertake further study of the process and the problems.

CHAPTER 1

Bargaining in Education

What will my salary be? How long is the workday? What fringe benefits are connected with this job? Will I be able to observe religious holidays? These and similar questions are matters of concern to all who are employed. Regardless of the dedication one brings to a job, everyone has a legitimate interest in the extent to which his job responsibilities affect him in life.

Until the recent past, boards of education decided these issues according to their best judgment and notified teachers and other employees of their obligations. Recently, however, teachers have asked for the right to participate in making these decisions. One way in which this participation can be accomplished is through collective negotiations. The purpose of this first chapter is to explore briefly the nature of this process, how it came to be used in American public education, and some consequences of this new development.

THE NATURE OF COLLECTIVE BARGAINING

During the decade 1960–1970, many teachers in the United States turned to collective bargaining as a process for resolving issues between themselves and their employers. Before that history is examined, some consideration of this tool for the resolution of disputes is in order.

Historically, the individual worker felt himself to be powerless in the face of his employer. The work relationship is partially a matter of buying and selling services. For the most part, employers were able to substitute one employee for another at relatively little cost. The unhappy employee, throughout time, was dependent upon the good nature, or the willingness to listen to reason, of the employer. The employee could rarely threaten the employer in any meaningful way by refusing to work, since normally the employer could easily replace him. Since quitting often hurt the employee more than the employer, the employee had little recourse when he was dissatisfied with the conditions of his employment.

The Impact of Collective Bargaining

The possibility of concerted action by all employees redressed this balance. When employees could agree on demands, and agree on concerted action to enforce their demands, the employer was faced with the potential loss of a vital element of production, his labor force. This imposed a potential cost of disagreement on the employer and established a rough balance of power. Potential damage requires the employer to pay attention to the concerns of employees.

For a long time, collective action of this sort was held in common law to be an illegal conspiracy against employers. Courts could and did forbid and punish attempts at joint action. Early in the twentieth century, however, this doctrine eroded. In the era of the New Deal, it was replaced by legislation specifically authorizing collective action by employees.

A Legal Basis

The National Labor Relations Act of 1935, known as the Wagner Act, and the companion legislation in 1947, commonly termed the Taft-Hartley Act, established and then confirmed the position of the Congress that the public interest was served by guaranteeing workers certain rights to collective action in pursuit of their interests as employees. This legislation applied only to interstate commerce. It did, however, mark a change in public attitude that has been reflected in similar legislation for intrastate commerce, and later for public employees.

Employee rights guaranteed by legislation can be summarized as follows:

1. To organize independent unions to represent them in dealings with employers.
2. To be free from the threat of having unions dominated by, dependent upon, or subservient to the employer.
3. To be free from discrimination by employers for interest in unions through discharge or other means.
4. To be guaranteed protection against retaliation by employers for testifying or participating in proceedings.
5. To engage in bargaining through legally established unions.

The exercise of these rights has established the process called collective bargaining. The Taft-Hartley Act defines this process in this way:

To bargain collectively is the performance of the mutual obligation of the employer and the representative of the employees to meet at reasonable times and confer in good faith with respect to wages, hours, and other terms and conditions of employment, or the negotiation of an agreement or any question arising there-under and the execution of a written contract incorporating any agreement reached if requested by either party, but such obligation does not compel either party to agree to a proposal or to require the making of a concession.[1]

Analysis of this language, and of the precedents established by interpretations of the statute in specific disputes, has established the basic nature of the collective-bargaining process.

Employers are required to negotiate on certain matters. This means that they cannot make decisions about those matters without achieving the agreement of the representative of the employees *prior to* announcing the decision. And it implies that the representative of the employees may block the decision until it is ready to give its assent.

Employees are authorized to propose changes in the work relationship. Employers must listen to these proposals and, at the very least, must respond with a thorough explanation of why they cannot reasonably comply with the demand.

Collective representation is mandated. Employees are not authorized to deal directly with their employer on bargainable items. The collective-bargaining process is based upon an agreement developed between the employer and the *representative* of the employees. Thus, wages, hours, and conditions of employment are determined for employees by agreement between unions and employers and not directly by employees themselves.

All agreements resulting from negotiations must be expressed in writing so that a specified basis for the employment relationship is recorded and communicated in a similar form to all who are affected by it.

THE DEVELOPMENT OF BARGAINING IN PUBLIC EMPLOYMENT

Collective bargaining developed more slowly in public employment than in the private sector. Broad-based public opinion that collective action by government employees was contrary to public welfare

1. Labor Management Relations Act (Taft-Hartley Act), 301 (a) 61 Stat. 156. (1947), 29 U.S.C. 185 (a) (1964).

appears to have been the major reason. Organizations of public employees traditionally sought to further the interests of their members through lobbying to produce legislation favorable to their interests rather than demanding collective-bargaining rights.

Public-school teachers are a good example. Legislation in the various states established job-security provisions through tenure laws, provided for exemplary retirement programs by statute. In many cases laws established statewide minimum salary schedules, and sometimes even guaranteed annual increments. All of these might have been objectives sought through bargaining, but instead they were achieved through legislation.

Strikes in Public Employment

With but few exceptions, the right to strike has been denied public employees. Since strikes are attempts to inflict damage upon the employer and hence coerce the employer into agreements, most states refuse to authorize such action. Many states, to the contrary, specifically prohibit strikes by public employees. Some have severe punishments expressed in the law.

Some argue, however, that the strike is the only means by which employee organizations can compel public employers to bargain realistically. They hold that public agencies will simply go through the motions of bargaining unless they can be embarrassed or damaged in some way when no agreement is reached. Those holding this position argue that teachers may be so provoked by unreasonable boards of education as to be goaded into strike action in defiance of the law. They say that boards are tempted, even encouraged, to be adamant in refusing legitimate teacher demands by being led to believe that strikes will not occur because they are illegal. This belief, and the resultant miscalculation of teacher determination, it is held, may well lead, paradoxically, to a greater likelihood of strikes where they are forbidden than would be the case where their authorization resulted in meaningful collective bargaining. This, or similar reasoning, has been instrumental in establishing a limited legalization of strikes by teachers and some other public employees in a few states.

Essential Public Services

Those who would prohibit strikes by public employees argue that public services are public because of their importance to the general welfare. If certain services are so critical to the functioning of our society, they maintain, it is foolish to permit them to be interrupted in order for employees to advance their private interest. While those private interests are important, they are not as important as the public interest which caused the original establishment of these services. The armed forces, police and fire departments, and welfare services are often cited as particularly dramatic examples of instances where human danger and misery result from interruption of service.

The advocates of a limited right to strike for public employees counter these arguments. Often, they concede, strikes in such areas do perhaps need to be prohibited. They then go on to point out that other public services are not nearly so clearly related to public safety or potential distress. Libraries, street maintenance, and parks are noted as forms of public employment where a temporary interruption in service is even less damaging to the public welfare than some legal strikes in private employment. Even schools, it has been pointed out, close for a number of reasons, varying from sudden snow storms to teacher-conference days, without detriment to students.

Bargaining in Federal Employment

The movement toward collective bargaining in public employment received a big push in 1962 when President Kennedy established Executive Order 10988. The impact of this order was to require that certain employee rights be extended to those employed by the federal government. The rights included:

1. The right of employees to join organizations of their choice.
2. Organizations could be granted informal, formal, or exclusive recognition.
3. The executive of the agency is required to meet and confer with respect to personnel policies and working conditions.
4. Advisory arbitration of grievances arising under the operation of agreements resulting from such meet-and-confer sessions must be provided for.

The order further established that any organization that asserts the right to strike against the government, and organizations that discriminate in any form against any employee, must be denied recognition. Once this order was in force, there was rapid movement in developing collective bargaining in federal employment. And, as employees indicated their wish to be represented collectively, unions of government workers flourished.

Decision in Connecticut

The teachers of Norwalk, Connecticut, attempted to organize and to engage in collective bargaining with the board of education through a series of activities from 1946 through 1951. These culminated in a decision by the Connecticut Supreme Court of Errors, June term, 1951. In that decision the court dealt with the general question of whether a board of education has the authority to engage in collective bargaining with its employees if it so desires. A number of related questions were adjudicated at the same time.

The decision generally said yes. The court specifically rejected the right of the teacher organization to strike to force such negotiations. It made it clear that an organization was only empowered to bargain on behalf of its members. The court said that full authority to make decisions rested with the board of education and that the board could not delegate responsibilities placed upon it by statute. The court responded to a subquestion by indicating that the two parties could agree to arbitrate disputes arising between them so long as this was done voluntarily by both board and association. And the court determined that the association had no right to establish rules governing working conditions, but that all rule-making authority resided with the board of education. However, subject to those limitations, the court agreed that if the board determined that collective negotiation was the method by which it would establish wages, hours, and conditions of employment for some of its employees, nothing in Connecticut law forbade such action.

New York Sets a Pattern

Norwalk established legal precedent. But most teachers in the United States were unaware of, and perhaps largely uninterested in, collective negotiations until the early sixties. Probably the most important single happening was the winning of bargaining rights by the United Federation of Teachers in New York City.

This event was marked by a strike. The teachers demanded that the board of education accept the principle of collective bargaining and provide for a means of determining who should represent teachers in such negotiations. The board first agreed in principle to negotiations, and then later, after continued pressure, established a basis by which an election was held. The purpose of this election was to enable teachers to choose their bargaining agent.

At the time of the election, there were a large number of teacher organizations in New York. The United Federation of Teachers was relatively small. However, the federation won an overwhelming victory in the election and emerged as the exclusive representative of teachers in the New York City schools for negotiations to determine wages, hours, and terms and conditions of employment.

In this one action, well over 30,000 teachers entered into a new relationship with their employer. From that point on the teachers of New York City would have a representative meeting on equal footing with the board of education to work out a mutually satisfactory agreement. Interest in collective bargaining flared throughout the metropolitan school systems of the country.

The Battle for Representation Rights

Collective negotiation requires employee organizations to serve as the advocate for employees. Bargaining takes place between the employer and the representative of the employees. Teachers, if they are to bargain, need agents to represent them.

In theory, almost anyone not subservient to the employer could represent an employee group. In practice, employees almost always prefer that their agent be some organization made up at least in part of themselves. Unions and employee associations are such organizations. They exist for the express purpose of representing groups of employees in their dealings with their employers.

In the early sixties, local and state organizations affiliated with the National Education Association enrolled the vast preponderance of American teachers who belonged to any employee group. While membership in the NEA itself was far short of membership in the local and state affiliates, still the NEA far exceeded any other national teacher organization.

The American Federation of Teachers, AFL-CIO, had been in existence since 1919. Its membership for many decades was a small group of dedicated members who believed that the needs of teachers required unionization. Most of these members were in metropolitan school systems. They were ignored by most teachers, however. In 1960, 60,000 teachers were members of the AFT. In that same year, nearly 714,000 teachers belonged to the NEA. Affiliated state and local membership figures were much larger still.

But surprises were in store. Early on, for instance, an election was held in Philadelphia to determine who would represent teachers in the newly developing collective-negotiations relationships in that city. At the time the election was held, the Philadelphia Education Association had over 5,000 members, the Philadelphia Federation of Teachers, about 500 members. Approximately 10,500 teachers were employed in the city. To the surprise of many, the Philadelphia Federation of Teachers was chosen by a vote of 5,403 to 4,671. Clearly, teachers join organizations for differing purposes. Organizations preferred as the bargaining representatives may not be the ones to which people belong at the time of the election. Later elections in other major cities confirmed the trend to union representation for teachers. This threat became a matter of great concern to the NEA. It responded vigorously, and a hard-fought battle for representation rights and membership ensued between the two organizations.

Exceptions exist. However, in general, the teacher unions organized under the AFT banner were very successful in organizing and winning representation rights in the major metropolitan cities, especially in the Northeast. Some school districts located close to those cities joined in the trend. However, the rapid string of successes of the AFT affiliates slowed after the major cities were won. The NEA was successful in maintaining its traditional membership base within smaller communities.

While this competition was at its strongest, and under the press of that competition, the NEA became a different organization. Its public statements became more militant, classroom teachers clearly became the dominant power, and administration affiliates became much less influential. By the end of the sixties, fewer important differences remained between AFT and NEA.

In the early days, the NEA had held that all professionals engaged in education had common concerns and that the concept of a unified profession, which included administrators as well as classroom teachers, ought to be preserved. The AFT consistently held that a basic difference of concern and responsibility existed, and restricted its membership to classroom teachers.

The NEA has held that collective bargaining in education needs to develop its own procedures and precedents to take into account the specialized nature of bargaining in education. It has held that disputes ought to be settled by some means other than labor-relations boards. The AFT has supported the position that bargaining in education is basically the same process as bargaining in any sphere, and that labor laws and labor mechanisms serve the interests of teachers.

The Movement toward Merger

As the conflict over representation rights and membership lessened, and as the philosophical distinctions between the organizations became blurred, some began to think in terms of the mutual benefits to be gained by merging the two organizations into a single powerful voice of American teachers. Arguments about the destructive waste of resources in fighting each other, and seductive thoughts of becoming perhaps the most powerful and best financed union in the United States, have led to tentative steps toward eventual consolidation.

The leadership of the AFT has gone further than the NEA in suggesting such a move. The AFT gained a great deal of membership strength from 1965 to the early seventies, but its ranks still include slightly less than a half-million teachers. The NEA, partly as a result of its drive for unified membership, now exceeds a million members.

A major movement toward unification came when New York teachers, under the leadership of the charismatic Al Shanker of the UFT, agreed to merge their organizations. The 1973 convention of the NEA moved more slowly than advocates had hoped to expand this action into a national merger. Yet the issue is very much before both organizations, and further consideration appears assured.

The implications of merger are awesome. Assuming broad support by the existing membership of both organizations, a formidable political power would be created. The NEA presently is one of the world's largest employee organizations. Merger suggests a mammoth union indeed. Only the teamsters and the auto-workers unions would be of comparable size. In addition, a close cooperative working relationship already exists between the NEA and the American Federation of State, County, and Municipal Employees. And this is the fastest-growing union in the nation, presently exceeding a half-million membership.

The American Federation of Labor, Congress of Industrial Organizations, has developed a political arm called the Committee on Political Education (COPE). The National Education Association has a counterpart, the Political Action Committee for Education (PACE). Both organizations clearly mean to use their potential for political clout to elect legislators and executives friendly to their interests. With or without merger, it appears certain that the voice of organized teachers will be a major political force in the immediately foreseeable future.

TEACHERS AND THEIR EMPLOYERS

Collective bargaining is a means by which the disputes between employers and employees are resolved. The nature of the employment relationship in any given field gives clues to the nature of the disputes and hence the applicability of collective bargaining in a given instance. Teaching is one vocation within which notable changes in the nature of the employment relationship have taken place recently.

Employment as a Teacher in Earlier Times

Until recently most school districts in the United States were small sociopolitical entities marked by close interpersonal relationships. In 1930, over 125,000 separate school districts existed in our country. So many districts meant that most of them were quite small.

Paternalism has recently been used as a sneer term In these intimate districts, however, it was natural. The members of a board of education were generally the respected elders of the community. Virtually all members of the teaching staff were permanent residents of the community. A large proportion had themselves grown up in the community and attended its schools. In a very real sense, both students and teachers were the children of the community. The members of the boards of education normally had strong parental feelings of responsibility for the welfare of both. From the viewpoint of the individual teacher, if a parent or an uncle was not actually a member of the school board, at least one member was a close friend of a relative. Obedience and acceptance of the authority of the board in such a circumstance was inevitable.

Reinforcing these authority and obedience relationships was the fact that teaching was a feminized profession in an age when feminism meant acquiescence to male authority, at least in legal, business, and political relationships. The teacher, as an employee, was thus constrained by powerful social, economic, and familial forces to accept quietly the fortunes of his or her employment. And indeed, the existing order of things was so ingrained that few even thought to question its propriety.

District Reorganization

At least three factors appear to have played a significant role in the movement during the thirties and forties to consolidate school districts into fewer and larger systems. The world had been moving from a predominantly agricultural economy to an industrialized one for some time. The need for broader curriculums was becoming more and more apparent. High schools, particularly, found that adequate breadth of subject matter to meet new demands required larger enrollments. Improved roads and modern buses made transportation of students practicable. And the increased costs of new educational programs led to the realization that an adequate tax base was essential for every school district.

The number of school districts declined rapidly throughout the middle of this century. By 1973 only slightly more than 17,000 school districts remained. During the same time, the population of the country nearly doubled. The small, everybody-knows-everybody-else school district became a rarity.

Changes in Teachers

Changes were simultaneously occurring in the composition of teaching staffs. During the first quarter of this century, a large proportion of teachers entered the profession with a two-year normal-school preparation. Twenty-five years later, virtually every state required a four-year undergraduate degree for basic certification. Master's degrees were held by only a few, mostly administrators, until the recent past. Now many teachers, in most schools, have preparation matching that of their supervisors. Recent statistics demonstrate the influx of men into the teaching profession. In 1972, 34 percent of all public-school teachers were men. Secondary school particularly has been affected by this development.

As one puts these facts together, a picture of revolutionary change appears. School districts have become larger. With growth has come more formalized bureaucratic organization, where in defined rules have supplanted, to a large extent, the individualized treatment of individual requests. Boards of education, formerly small-scale employers of a few locally oriented teachers with whom they had direct personal and social contact, have been transformed into employers of large faculties that include many teachers who have no emotional ties to that particular community. Teachers, with increased education, freely question the decisions of their supervisors. Males, responsible for providing for their families, often have greater demands upon their paycheck and hence are increasingly conscious of financial pressures.

Climate of Militancy

All of these changes, crowding one upon the other, brought about important changes in the way many teachers looked at themselves and their jobs. One additional factor was important. Militancy was in the air during the sixties. Civil-rights movements struggled to end racial discrimination, first in the South and later throughout our nation. Vietnam became a festering sore dividing the young from their parents, hawks from doves, and those who had served from those whose consciences did not permit them to support what they believed to be an unjust war. Those who trusted the institutions of our society found themselves at odds with those who saw those institutions as instruments of betrayal.

Demonstrations designed to communicate through the mass media were used by believers of all stripes. Universities, churches, government operations were disrupted. Cities exploded into violence. Reasonable discourse between those with differing opinions became difficult. An existentialist belief that one must choose and then act to demonstrate commitment led many from argument to conflict over these critical social and political issues.

Teachers were involved in all of these struggles. In their involvement they came, more and more, to accept the belief that open, organized conflict to secure one's ends was preferable to conflict avoidance. When boards of education hesitated to grant demands for bargaining rights, many teachers accepted militant action as the normal response to an opposing force. Teacher unions became more aggressive. Associations moved toward union positions to avoid the taint of Uncle Tomism. Rarely in our history had the collective temper of our society been so short.

The Teacher's Dilemma

Issues of employment relations create special difficulties for teachers because of a dichotomy in the nature of their job. Teachers are, at the same time, both professionals and employees.

The difficulty in that arrangement is illuminated, perhaps, by the comparisons that frequently are made by teachers between themselves and physicians. Teachers are told that they are professionals and have obligations and ethical responsibilities based upon that professionalism. So, teachers say, Why are we not accorded the same status and freedom of operation which exists for the medical and legal professions?

Reflection, however, leads to realization of an important distinction. Most professionals work on a fee-for-services-rendered basis over a relatively short term with individuals who have sought their services. When one is dissatisfied with a physician or attorney, one can go to someone else. Medical or bar associations help to protect people against incompetence. But the primary protection of the individual lies in his ability to go elsewhere.

Teachers, on the other hand, are employed by the public at large to staff what is, for most children, the only real opportunity for formal education. To be sure, some families can choose private schools if the public school displeases them. But this choice is real for only a small number of citizens.

The employment relationship is not between the teacher as an individual and the parent, but rather between teachers as a group and society as a whole. A monopoly exists. Where a monopoly exists, society depends upon controls to protect its interests.

In the case of public education, the control is exercised by placing decision-making power in the hands of a board of education sworn to secure and advance the public interest. Teachers are, and ought to be, recognized as professionals. But they are not independent fee-taking professionals. They are professionals in public service. That is, they are also employees of the public. As employees, they are expected to submit to the discipline and authority of the board. Considerable professional judgment must be exercised if teaching is to be effective. But if schools are to be public schools, that judgment must be exercised within the constraints established by the public's representatives. These are expressed in public schools through policy enacted by the board of education and binding upon all employees.

Collective bargaining is a means by which employees can participate in a realistic way in the development of board-of-education policy determining wages, hours, and terms and conditions of employment. It is important to keep in mind two important points. The product of successful collective bargaining is policy to which both the board and the representative of the teachers consent. And once the policy has been so developed and ratified, it is equally binding upon both parties.

SUMMARY

Collective bargaining is a process developed in the United States. It is unique to our society and similar Western democracies. It is a new tool, and one which we are still learning to use. The basic concept is that employees should be granted rights to organize and to be represented by agents of their choice in determining the basic conditions of their employment. This concept was first applied to industry in interstate commerce. Within the past few years, collective bargaining, or collective negotiations, as it is frequently called in education, has been extended more and more to public employment, including public schools and colleges.

The history of public education in this country and the nature of the teaching-learning relationship are important considerations, which make the study of collective bargaining in education more than an extension of conventional labor-relations theory. The relationship between the citizen and the teacher of his children encompasses both the intimacy of parental concerns and the complexity of political considerations for the management of the largest single enterprise of our nation.

CHAPTER 2

Organizing and Operating Collectively

The concept of employees bargaining collectively with their employer to determine the conditions of their employment was only the starting point. Before employees could benefit from the idea, a means by which all of this could be done had to evolve. The intent of this chapter is to explain how employees do operate collectively. Most of these means came about as the requirements of the Wagner Act were implemented in business and industry following the enactment of that legislation. In public employment the precedents and conventions have largely, but not entirely, been borrowed from that industrial experience.

The passage of the Wagner Act brought about the establishment of the National Labor Relations Board. The responsibility of this board was to serve as an umpire in collective bargaining between employer and employee. The specific requirements of the law as it applied to specific instances had to be decided. Most statutes look to court decisions to illuminate the specifics of the law. Labor disputes can and do go to the courts for resolution, but many disputes are settled by decisions of the National Labor Relations Board. These decisions have established a vast set of precedents which guide later decisions of the board as well as those of courts. As the several states followed the lead of the Congress and passed laws requiring bargaining in businesses and industries engaged in intrastate commerce, they also established state labor-relations bodies to fulfill this same function. Later, as states established laws requiring bargaining by public employers, some established separate boards and commissions to oversee collective bargaining in the public sector. Others added this task to the charge of the existing state labor-relations bodies.

One of the outcomes of decisions by these agencies has been to define with greater clarity just what the employer must do in order to avoid engaging in an unfair labor practice. Organizations of employees are also required to obey the rules established by these commissions. So the network of related rulings and orders of the various labor boards, together with the law itself, make up the body of labor law in this country. A branch of the legal profession exists to assist clients in the understanding and interpretation of this mass of regulations.

THE BARGAINING UNIT

The term *collective* emphasizes that bargaining as used in this book refers only to the creation of understandings between the employer and *groups of employees.* Before anything can be done to bring about collective negotiations, the specific group to which any agreements will apply must be established. It must be possible to determine whether any single employee is or is not included in this group. The term applied to the established group is the *bargaining unit.*

The bargaining unit is a group of positions within an organization rather than a group of people. That is, an individual employee is a member of the bargaining unit so long as he holds a position which has been included in it. If an employee is transferred to another position not in the defined unit, he is no longer affected by the agreement covering the unit. In the case of teachers, a teacher belonging to a bargaining unit of classroom teachers would be covered by an agreement only so long as that position was held. If that teacher should become a principal, for instance, or perhaps a department head, and *if* these positions were not included in the bargaining unit, he would cease to be covered in any way by the existing agreement. The negotiated contract is negotiated on behalf of, and applies to, those holding a group of positions previously agreed to as constituting the bargaining unit.

Determining the Unit

The decision as to which positions are in the bargaining unit and which are not has important implications. Where collective negotiations are not required by law, a board of education can bargain or refuse to bargain at its own discretion. The decision as to whom to include in a bargaining unit is similarly at its discretion. Where a board is required by law to bargain, however, the story may be quite different. It may be that the board and the teachers can agree between themselves as to which positions should be included. If so, fine, no problem.

Where they disagree, but are required by law to bargain, this disagreement must be resolved before the requirement to bargain can be fulfilled. Some agency must rule. Generally the state labor board or public-employee commission serves that function.

Two considerations are apt to guide this decision: *community of interest* and *fragmentation*. Community of interest as a criterion reflects the necessity for the employees in a bargaining unit to have generally similar employment concerns and interests. The agreement will affect all in the bargaining unit in the same way. If the employees are not much alike in their employment circumstances, it is difficult to draft an agreement which can be applied fairly to all. Even elementary teachers and high-school teachers may have differences that could cause difficulty in establishing an agreement that would apply fairly to both. But generally such differences can be overcome. On the other hand, teachers and bus drivers, for instance, are usually not included in the same unit because such issues as hours required in the workday normally need different resolution for each.

If bargaining units were very small, community of interest would be easier to maintain. But very small units are disliked by employees and employers alike. Employees fear small units since a disagreement with only a few employees is not much more damaging to the employer than a disagreement with an individual. The power of employees acting collectively is dissipated. Employers, too, find that fragmentation of their work force into many separate bargaining units is unsatisfactory since it requires the employer to bargain many times, generally over the same questions, but with different groups of employees.

So those attempting to determine the makeup of a bargaining unit try to form one that is as large as possible without mixing of employees with disparate concerns. At the same time, they try to keep the unit small enough for homogeneity without being so small as to risk fragmentation.

The Teacher as a Unit Member

Once a unit is formed, the teacher included in it relates to the board of education in new and importantly different ways. But these new relationships apply only in a limited field. Various state laws requiring bargaining may define these a bit differently. Frequently, however, terminology is borrowed from the Wagner Act. Bargaining is required for the determination of wages, hours, and terms and conditions of employment. Hence, these employment relationships of the individual to his employer are changed. All other relationships remain as they were.

This is a big difference, however. How much each teacher is paid will be decided through agreement between those representing all in the bargaining unit and the employer. The hours one is required to work are similarly so determined. Matters included under the umbrella phrase "other terms and conditions of employment" are likewise so decided. Special considerations and exceptions by the employer are frowned upon and may well constitute unfair labor practices. All in the unit must be treated alike. A single agreement must be established which applies to all.

Many teachers find this concept difficult to accept. They are used to thinking in terms of the individual differences and individual needs of pupils. In accordance with their training, teachers generally operate, insofar as possible, to modify treatment given to pupils in accordance with their differences. Many, especially those teaching in smaller schools, are themselves accustomed to asking for and receiving special consideration for special circumstances. Teachers, in the past, were able to work out understandings with principals or superintendents. When teachers refer to humanizing the schools, they are often thinking of just these kinds of special considerations.

While some of this may persist in schools in which collective bargaining exists, clearly it is antithetical to the concept of collective agreements. Teachers cannot expect to receive the benefits of collective action without paying the price of loss of individual autonomy and individualized treatment. A contract or agreement is negotiated to cover all members of a bargaining unit. It is to apply to all members equally. Teacher organizations and school administrators must uphold this principle, even though they may sometimes regret the inability to respond to individual needs.

Faced with this, teachers sometimes ask to be excused from membership in the bargaining unit and continue to relate as an individual with the employer. Such requests cannot be granted. Once a bargaining unit has been established, its makeup can be changed only by the agency that established it, and only if the nature of a position has so changed as to make it no longer compatible with the community of interest of others in the unit. The individual teacher may not decide whether or not to be represented in collective bargaining.

A BARGAINING AGENT

Once the bargaining unit has been established, an agent must be chosen to represent those who are included within it. Collective bargaining takes place between an employer and the *representative* of the employees. Employees, as individuals, have no right to engage in bargaining directly.

Selecting an Agent

Theoretically, the bargaining agent could be almost anyone designated by the members of the bargaining unit. In practice, an organization of employees usually fulfills the role. This organization is normally termed a union, although in education the affiliates of the NEA have preferred to continue to be termed associations.

One of the basic rights of employees is the right to freely choose their representative for collective-bargaining purposes. A number of regulations and precedents serve to guarantee that right and restrict the actions of employers in order that employee freedom of choice be guaranteed. In education, principals or other admininstrators can express a preference or a belief that one or another possible bargaining agent or union might be preferable. But the actions of representatives of the board must carefully avoid any taint of coercion or threat. Teachers or other employees must be free to select whomever they prefer to be their spokesman in collective bargaining.

While several means have been used to determine that choice, a secret-ballot election is preferable in most instances. Where an election is held, the right to vote is extended only to those who are members of the bargaining unit and hence whose representative the winner will be. Election procedures must be carefully planned to insure that only those entitled to vote receive a ballot, that they are accurately informed prior to voting, that ballots are carefully preserved and counted, and, in general, that fair election practices are followed by both employers and the various groups that may be contending for representation rights. The winner is certified as the bargaining agent for the bargaining unit and continues in that position until some future date when the members of the bargaining unit may decide to hold another election.

The most widely accepted form of representation is called exclusive representation. A teachers' organization must receive a majority of the votes cast in order to be so designated. The exclusive representative speaks for all employees in the bargaining unit, regardless of whether or not a given individual is a member of that organization. A teacher, for instance, may choose to belong to an NEA affiliate, but be in a bargaining unit in which the AFT has exclusive representation rights. That teacher can be represented only by the AFT. Conversely, the AFT must represent that teacher even though he is not a member of the union and pays no dues for representation services.

Some states have forms of multiple representation designed to preserve the freedom of individual teachers to choose their representative. The difficulty of conducting collective bargaining with multiple bargaining agents has kept this practice from gaining widespread adoption, however.

Power and Authority of the Agent

As implied above, being selected as a bargaining agent confers both responsibilities and powers on a union or association. Since the agreement will be between the bargaining agent and the employer, the individual teacher becomes subject to the decisions of these powerful agencies. While the teacher has some control over the decisions of the association or union, that control, in practical terms, is limited to choosing officers who, one hopes, will make the kinds of decisions one prefers in determining wages, hours, and conditions of employment. The bargaining agent may, and usually does, include in the agreement with the employer some guarantees that serve to strengthen its power and security as an organization.

From the standpoint of the individual teacher, any one of four possible circumstances may be present. (1) He may be a member of the bargaining unit (by virtue of the position he holds as an employee) and also a member of the organization chosen as the bargaining agent. (2) He may be a member of the bargaining unit but not of the organization that represents it. (3) He may not be included in the bargaining unit as it is defined because of the nature of the position he holds, but for social or ideological reasons still holds membership in the union (department chairmen sometimes do this). (4) Finally, he may be an employee of a given school district, but is not included in the bargaining unit and does not choose to belong to the organization representing that unit.

Concerns of Teachers, Unions, and School Boards

As collective bargaining takes place, one can expect the somewhat divergent interests of three groups to become evident. The teacher predictably wants improvements in his employment circumstances. Higher salaries, eased requirements of the job, improved physical conditions are all legitimate demands that members of the unit will expect to have advanced by their representative. The bargaining agent, union, or association will also have concerns. The maintenance of its mandate as the representative of the unit will be a major objective. It is also necessarily concerned with the size of its membership, the collection of dues, and the costs of operation since these, in concert, establish its financial position. Some issues may be desired by the membership of the unit but feared by the bargaining agent because implementation would lead to high operating costs. Finally, administration is primarily concerned with operating the schools. This concern is often reflected in two ways. Administration always fears long-term guarantees since its ability to finance the guarantees may change. And administration is properly concerned that its flexibility to change as situations change not be unduly compromised.

An Adversary Relationship

Collective bargaining is based upon a presumption that the best interests of the general public are served when the selfish interests of the parties to the employment relationship are resolved through negotiation rather than by other means. Collective bargaining does not presume that selfish interests will not exist, nor does it hold that they ought to be disregarded. Quite the contrary. The bargaining agent representing teachers exists solely to articulate and try to achieve the goals determined to be in the self-interest of its members. The welfare of the school as an institution may, in fact, be advanced by teacher organizations seeking to achieve the interests of teachers. But that is a by-product. The bargaining agent represents teachers and their interests. The collective-bargaining process is predicated upon the union or association being an advocate of a special-interest group—the members of the bargaining unit.

Assumptions of Compatibility and Conflict

On the other hand, the board of education and its agents, the admininstration of the school, are charged with representing the interests of the public. Both the interest in having the best possible education for children and the interest in having that education provided at the lowest possible cost are legitimate. Collective bargaining assumes that the self-interest of teachers and the concerns of the public, expressed through the board, will be compatible in the long run. It assumes that teachers desire that public education continue to exist and be operated through present institutions. It assumes that boards will govern, that administration will administer, and that teachers will be employees of the schools. But collective bargaining also assumes that in the short run, sharp differences of opinion will exist as to how the enterprise should be operated and how available funds should be allocated.

Significance of a Balance of Power

Laws requiring collective bargaining normally attempt to establish and preserve a balance of power. If either party, employee organization or employer, is sufficiently powerful to insist upon its own way, presumably it will do so, at least in matters it deems important. Where that is the case, bargaining will not take place, or if it does it will only be a sham. Collective bargaining works when neither the teacher organization nor the board of education can have its own way. Then each is placed in a position where it must gain the assent of the other if the mutually desired continuation of public education is to be possible. The act of collective bargaining is a search by both parties for a middle ground which is as favorable to its own interest as possible but is acceptable to the other party. This means that agreements arrived at through negotiations will be less than fully satisfactory to either side. Both will wish for more than they receive. But collective bargaining, in the presence of a balance of power, can result in an agreement with which both parties feel they can live, and which both parties voluntarily accept as preferable to any other basic agreement and as preferable to no agreement at all.

UNFAIR LABOR PRACTICES

Laws requiring collective negotiations and interpretations of those laws by labor-relations boards and courts have created a host of rulings, regulations, and precedents which require or restrict action by both employers and organizations representing employees. Because these laws were designed to require employers to relate to their employees in new ways, most of the restrictions are on the employer—in this case, the board of education. Violations of the regulations are commonly termed *unfair labor practices.*

In a state in which bargaining between a board of education and the representative of teachers is required, and unfair labor practice normally is determined by the state labor-relations board or public employment commission. Usually, a charge of unfair practice is brought by an individual or organization which feels that a certain action of the board violates one or more of the rules. In the normal course of things, such an allegation would be filed with the appropriate agency. The agency would conduct such hearings or investigations as it felt to be necessary and would then issue an order requiring the board to cease and desist if it found the charge to be well grounded. Since the labor board or similar agency acts as an instrument of the state in enforcing state legislation, such a finding must be either obeyed or appealed. If an appeal is desired by either party, it is made to an appropriate court of law.

In common parlance, an unfair labor practice appears to be any action that an adversary in the collective-bargaining process objects to. A fair amount of newspaper coverage can sometimes be gained by such charges, and since public opinion is important in bargaining, the parties are tempted to play to that gallery. In order to be sustained, however, a charge of unfair labor practice must be tied specifically to a requirement of the law.

Restrictions on Boards of Education

Five restrictions on boards of education are found in many state codes. The first is that employers may not interfere with, restrain, or coerce employee in their exercise of rights granted by the law. Thus, a refusal to grant tenure to an individual, stemming from his aggressive leadership in the teacher organization, would be an action forbidden to a board of education. To be sure, an incompetent teacher may be refused tenure regardless of his actions in a union. But the board must be especially careful to insure that the reasons for such action are documented and are free from any suggestion that union activity was a related consideration. That can be especially difficult in a case, for instance, where zealotry in association business has resulted in a teacher's slighting of his responsibilities to his classes. A second restriction on the board is that it may not dominate the teacher organization. In private industry, "company unions" were sometimes found. These cozy relationships gave the employee a sense of representation without facing the employer with any real pressure. The restriction upon this means that the teacher organization must be fully independent of the board. In some cases, prior to the introduction of collective bargaining, cooperative boards permitted teacher organizations to use school equipment, supplies, and facilities without charge in an attempt to be cooperative. While teacher organizations may bargain for such usage, the implication of this restriction on the employer is that the board may not freely grant it, and should impose a reasonable cost or extract some benefit in return from the teacher group. Where members of the administration hold positions of leadership in teacher organizations, similar charges may be leveled against the board of education. A principal might, in some instances, be a member of an organization which bargains on behalf of teachers without any problem existing. If that principal served on the executive committee, however, the board of education might well be charged with an attempt to dominate, even though the board might not even be aware of that membership.

Third, boards may not encourage or discourage membership in teacher organizations by discrimination in hiring, promotion, tenure, or conditions of employment. This, too, is an attempt to insure that employers do not interfere with the full functioning of employee organizations by affecting the growth of their membership. A question during an employment interview as to whether a prospective teacher is, or intends to be, a member of a bargaining unit is proscribed by such regulations. Teachers must be free to join, or refrain from joining, unions or associations. Organizations must be free to recruit members within reasonable limits. Boards must not attempt to damage unions by reducing their membership and hence their financial and bargaining strength.

A fourth restriction on boards is that they may not practice any discrimination against an employee for filing charges or testifying against the board. Obviously, the other restrictions against a board would be empty if no one dared file an unfair-labor-practice charge. This restriction protects the right of teachers to protect their rights by exercising them.

The last requirement is perhaps the most difficult to define with precision. The board is forbidden to refuse to bargain collectively with teachers. That leaves the question, What must the employer do to meet the minimum requirements of engaging in collective bargaining? For now, a short response: The employer and the representative of employees are both required to try, in good faith, to reach an agreement. The complexities of this obligation will be discussed in more detail in the next chapter.

Restrictions on Employee Organizations

The fact that most allegations of unfair labor practice are filed against the employer results largely from the fact that employee organizations are trying to bring about changes in existing practices, and hence are challenging the ways employers behave. This should not mislead one, however. Employee organizations can, and sometimes do, commit unfair labor practices and are subject to specific restrictions on their conduct.

Unfair labor practices by employee organizations are more likely to occur during competition for representation rights between two or more unions. The concept that the individual worker must be free to choose his representative applies to restrict union behavior as it does management behavior. Acts of intimidation of employees and misrepresentation on the part of contending unions are forbidden.

Employee organizations are required to exhibit the same good faith efforts to reach an agreement as are employers. Since unions normally are the ones seeking the agreement, this is less frequently a basis for an unfair-labor-practices charge. But one should remember that the employer may find it necessary to approach the representative of the employees to seek some change in the conditions of employment. In such a case the union, like the employer, is required to meet at reasonable times, to confer, and to respond in quite the same good-faith fashion.

Sometimes the allegation of unfair labor practices arises from a belief that the union has not done its best to represent an individual employee in some issue. This is particularly likely to occur where the union is the exclusive representative. The obligations of this relationship include full representation of all employees in the bargaining unit regardless of whether or not they are members of the union. Allegations that unions do a better job of representing their members than they do of representing nonmembers lead to such charges. A related circumstance sometimes occurs where dissent exists within the union, with one group trying to wrest control from the existing leadership. Such disaffection does not relieve the union of its responsibility to provide full and vigorous representation to all in the bargaining unit. Charges that the union has failed to do so can provide the basis for unfair-labor-practices findings.

THE AGENT PREPARES FOR BARGAINING

Teacher organizations face difficult problems as they get ready to fulfill their responsibility of representing the bargaining unit in negotiations with the board. Much of the collective bargaining consists of proposals that the board of education either do things not presently being done, do things being done but do them better, or, sometimes, refrain from doing certain things. Thus, the initiative for developing the subject matter of negotiations generally, although not completely, rests naturally enough with the representative of the employees.

Deciding What to Bargain For

Associations or unions want to do a good job of representation, partly out of their own integrity and partly because a dissatisfied bargaining unit can, and presumably will, replace them with another agent if it is not satisfied with the outcome. The first task the organization faces, then, is determining two important, but difficult things. First, what do the members of the bargaining unit want? And second, how strong and widespread is that want?

Frequently, the answer to the first question is sought by inviting all members of the bargaining unit to submit suggestions for demands or proposals. Remember, the bargaining unit may well include teachers who are not members of the organization. Organizations may be less interested in the desires of nonmembers. But where an organization is the exclusive representative, it is required to represent all in the unit, members and nonmembers alike. Mass involvement is useful in that it gives an opportunity for all to participate. This has important implications for the bargaining agent, which is naturally concerned about its image. It may, however, create difficult problems in determining just what is meant by various proposals, which may come in all forms, from carefully thought out letters, to hastily scrawled, ambiguous notes.

Many proposals are similar, and these must be consolidated into a single proposal, a process that inevitably distorts them somewhat. Others may be mutually exclusive; to ask one would deny the other. Some proposals seem to the officers of the organization to be undesirable or unreasonable, and must be ignored. And, finally, some decision must be made as to how many proposals should be made, whether all of them should be advanced even though all could never be granted, or whether the organization would be in a stronger bargaining position if it comes to the bargaining table with only a relatively few items of high priority and tries to achieve them all. All these considerations test the degree to which the organization is responsive to the concerns of the membership of the bargaining unit and the degree to which it is able to communicate effectively with that membership.

The second question is even more difficult. Some demands clearly would be supported by all of the membership. Others, however, reflect the concerns of a portion of those in the bargaining unit but are of little or no interest to others. The importance of the community-of-interest principle in unit determination is manifest here. If the unit is quite homogeneous, less of this problem will be present. If it is disparate, more will ensue. Suppose, for instance, that the few vocational-education teachers at the high school have a special problem which is of great importance to them. Will the mass of teachers in the elementary schools be willing to support this demand? What if the demand is made and then teachers in the system say, publicly, that they do not feel it is very important? How would bargaining be affected? Perhaps it would be better not to advance the demand. But if it is not included in the proposals, the vocational-education teachers might form the nucleus of a let's-have-a-new-leadership movement. What to do? This is the dilemma of all representatives!

Some kind of decision-making process must be carried out by the leadership of the bargaining agent as it prepares to go to the table to meet with the representatives of the board of education. Eventually, a specific list of proposals is formulated.

Presenting the Proposals

One final step remains. Just how should the proposals be advanced. Some say that you never get all you ask for. The logic following from this view is to inflate the demands to allow for some shrinkage. Casual observation tells us that this is not uncommon. It carries a danger for the bargaining agent and its leadership, however. If demands are made high and settlement is considerably lower, dissidents in the organization may shout "Sell-out!" "Look what a little bit they settled for!" is a scary charge for any agent. The converse is dangerous too, though. Undoubtedly, compromise will have to be made. The adversary at the other side of the table will hardly be able to return to the board of education and confess, "I gave them everything they asked for." Some reduction will be demanded, no matter how reasonable the initial demand, to permit the other negotiator to demonstrate that he has fulfilled his mission. If the teacher demands are close to the minimum that must be achieved, little room remains for the give-and-take of negotiations. So care must be taken in the formulation of demands to insure that they are both clearly stated and tactically positioned.

THE BOARD PREPARES FOR BARGAINING

Meanwhile, those who will represent the board of education are doing their homework in preparation for negotiations. In some ways their job is simpler, since their constituency is only the few members of the board. The board's team will not initiate many proposals. The proposals they will advance usually result from difficulties in administering a previous agreement.

Planning a Response to Proposals

The larger part of the preparation of the board's team comes after the first meeting in which the demands of the representatives of the teachers are presented. They must analyse each of these demands in order to prepare a recommended response.

Part of the analysis is to establish the cost. Sometimes demands are described as noneconomic, suggesting that no financial costs are involved. Actually, few, if any, of the demands teacher organizations might make are costless. Even administrative time is costly since time spent on one thing is time not available for something else. Analysis must also establish the impact of agreement on the operation of the school so that total effects can be foreseen. Finally, the board will attempt to determine which of the demands are likely to be of higher priority and which are perhaps less important to the teacher representatives. It is, of course, important to the teacher representatives that these priorities be revealed only when a tactical advantage might be secured. For this reason, the final plans of the union must be kept secret even from its own membership in order that damaging leaks be avoided.

Deciding to Accept as Negotiable

Most important of all, the board team must decide what to agree to bargain about, and what to reject as not suitable for bargaining. Considerable misunderstanding and argument frequently exist between teachers and boards over this point. If the board is required to bargain by statute, the statute will specify some language such as "wages, hours, and terms and conditions of employment" as that which must be bargained about. Now "wages" is pretty clear-cut, and "hours" has a common meaning, but what about "terms and conditions of employment"?

A CENTRAL ISSUE: WHAT IS NEGOTIABLE?

A general principle of law is important here. A board of education has no inherent powers. As a creature of the state, it possesses only the powers specifically granted or reasonably implied by statute. Where a board exceeds these powers, its actions may be voided and deprived of legal standing. Since the law requiring bargaining stipulates areas of policy formation to be bargained over, by implication the board has no authority to bargain over any other area, whether it might like to or not. So the board and the administration must decide, as best they can, whether they are empowered to negotiate on any given demand.

The board must put all proposals or demands into one of three categories. There are items about which bargaining is mandatory.

There are items—matters in which legislation has already determined what is to be done—about which the board is forbidden to bargain. And there are items about which the board may bargain if it chooses but which it cannot be forced to negotiate about by the bargaining law.

The board must bargain to establish wages, hours, and terms and conditions of employment. If the first of these are clear, the third assuredly is not. The legislature, in choosing such language, must have meant that more than the first two are required subjects for negotiation. Beyond that the two parties must make their way with less guidance. An issue such as class size is an excellent example. From the standpoint of the board, the size of classes is a matter of deciding what quality of educational program is to be provided. Further, class size is an immensely expensive item; a small reduction in the size of classes becomes a terrific additional expense in operating the schools. The board will likely feel that the responsibility of determining class size must remain with them as the representatives of the community. They might argue that to do otherwise would be similar to Congress conceding to the Pentagon equality in deciding how big an army the nation should have.

Teachers, though, look at the issue quite differently. What, they ask, could be more a condition of employment in teaching than the number of pupils one is responsible for. As this number increases, the burden of the job increases. Since much of teaching is done away from the place of work—grading papers, for instance—class size is an even better determinant of the demands of the job than hours, which are specifically bargainable! Short of salary, probably no issue is of greater concern to teachers as they contemplate their job circumstances. Further, teachers want to be successful in working with students. Much of their satisfaction comes from seeing students perform well. And while research evidence is lacking, most teachers are convinced that smaller classes increase the likelihood of student success.

An important point must be made here. The reluctance to bargain over an issue is *not* the same thing as a reluctance to permit teachers to have some voice in the making of the decision. A board might well feel that teachers ought to have an opportunity to be heard in the process of making a decision on class size. Once the board agrees to bargain over it, however, it agrees that teachers will have an *equal voice*, and that no decision about this or any other issue can be made without teacher organization agreement.

Guidance from Precedent Decisions

Some assistance in determining what must be bargained about emerges over time. For instance, a board of education refuses to bargain on a matter of deep interest to the teacher organization. The organization, feeling that the board has violated the law, files an unfair-labor-practice allegation with the appropriate state agency. When that agency rules on the matter, or when its ruling is appealed to the courts and finally decided, precedent is formed. If it is determined that the given issue is not one about which a board must bargain, or if the opposite is decided, presumably any future question would be decided similarly. So both boards and teacher organizations learn from these decisions more specifically what the phrase "terms and conditions of employment" means in that state.

In many jurisdictions the concept of inherent management policy is upheld. In Pennsylvania, for instance, the law requiring bargaining in public employment not only uses the term but defines it in the statute. The reference is to those matters which, it is believed, must be reserved to employers in order for the basic functions of management to be performed. Pennsylvania law says:

Public employers shall not be required to bargain over matters of inherent managerial policy which shall include but shall not be limited to such areas of discretion or policy as the functions and programs of the public employer, standards of services, its overall budget, utilization of technology, the organizational structure and selection and direction of personnel.[1]

The intent of the legislature was to reserve these functions to the board of education or other public employers.

Perhaps the best one can say for certain is that this phrase, "terms and conditions of employment," probably does refer to the physical conditions under which the employees work. Issues of health and safety of the employee in the workplace undoubtedly are bargainable. This is rarely a problem for teachers, however. Beyond that, teacher organizations in each state will have to probe the boundaries of the law as it applies. Militant bargaining and test cases on a number of points will be required to determine the range of possible bargainable issues.

Areas of School-Board Discretion

A last question remains. There are issues about which the board may bargain but is not forced to do so under the law. That being the case, a classic answer becomes comprehensible. Someone has truly said that the issues to be bargained are determined through bargaining. Just as

1. Pennsylvania Public Employees Relations Act, S. 702 P.S. (1970).

in any other issue, the board may be persuaded of the desirability of including an item for bargaining even though the law does not force it to do so. Examination of agreements, particularly those in metropolitan school districts, leads inescapably to the conclusion that boards have bargained and included in their agreements many issues beyond what the law requires. Sometimes one may persuade his adversary of the essential rightness of his position. Sometimes one may achieve his adversary's agreement in return for a trade-off agreement to someting the adversary wants. Sometimes boards agree to bargain on issues about which they would rather not simply because the alternatives are even less desirable.

SUMMARY

Before teachers can bargain collectively, several preliminary things must be done. The group to be represented must be defined with precision. A bargaining agent must be chosen to represent that group. The nature of that representation, whether exclusive or otherwise, must be established.

The bargaining agent must decide what issues to advance on behalf of the group it represents. These must be prepared in such a form that their presentation leads to success in achieving at least part of the objectives. Arguments between the bargaining agent and the board of education about what matters must be bargained must be resolved. Both parties are then ready to send teams to the bargaining table to attempt to reach a mutually satisfactory agreement.

CHAPTER 3

At the Bargaining Table

Organizational relationships serve to prepare the way for collective bargaining to be consummated. Bargaining exists when the employer and the representative of the employees meet at reasonable times and confer in good faith over wages, hours, and other terms and conditions of employment. The purpose of this chapter is to explain what takes place during that drama, some of the reasons for typical actions, the problems of the protagonists, and what lies behind bargaining acts.

Collective bargaining requires time. The representatives of both parties meet face to face, try to achieve their goals, meet again, and strain, at considerable cost of time and energy, to negotiate a settlement. Rarely do those who are being represented understand the heavy demands the act of bargaining places upon their spokesmen. The importance of the issues to both parties, and the emotions that bargaining arouses, often masks imaginative and sensitive human interaction by the negotiators as each tries to fulfill his or her respective responsibilities.

Some view bluff as the key to bargaining. Some see bargaining as a form of debate in which each side marshals evidence to persuade the other. Some have analyzed collective bargaining as a group problem-solving process. And some see it as a form of legalized extortion in which those with power inflict their will upon others. Some evidence exists to support each of these views. Probably it is more realistic to say that all of these behaviors exist during some instances of collective bargaining. But whatever the form, the arena in which bargaining takes place is largely, but not entirely, across the bargaining table.

SELECTING THE BARGAINING TEAM

One final preparation must be made by both parties before the first meeting. A bargaining team must be selected. Sometimes bargaining is

40

undertaken by a single individual. But by far the more prevalent process is for both employees and employer to choose a group to represent them.

Three primary roles can be identified for each team. This is not to suggest that only three individuals comprise a team, although that may well be the case. But however many members are on a team, three functions must be identified and assigned if the team is to have the best chance for success.

Chief Negotiator

The key figure is the chief negotiator. This is the person who will quarterback the team during the negotiations. He will be the chief spokesman. Experienced bargaining groups maintain tight discipline and forbid anyone other than the chief negotiator to speak to the opposition during bargaining unless the chief negotiator asks to have a point presented. The reason for this convention is that it is important that one's adversary be faced with a unified position. If he can find areas of disagreement within the team he opposes, he will surely exploit those differences. So a single spokesman is used to emphasize that a single point of view represents the position of the bargaining team. The chief negotiator bears a heavy responsibility. Extreme care must be taken in selecting the individual to fulfill the role. Certainly he must be knowledgeable about the process of collective bargaining. Coolness under pressure, an ability to articulate a position clearly, a detailed knowledge of the group he represents, and the ability to generate confidence in his integrity on the part of the opposition are important criteria for choice. The last factor is especially important in light of the common phrase, "Would you buy a used car from this man?" Neither party is apt to come to agreement with one whom it distrusts. If the agreement one seeks is to be achieved, the opposition must be willing to agree.

Observer

A second role is that of observer. This may often be combined with the responsibility of financial analyst and adviser. An observer is charged with being a second pair of eyes and ears for the chief negotiator. The spokesman will be concentrating on what he is saying or about to say. This makes it difficult for him to listen carefully and spot slight changes in the way the other side responds or reacts. Yet careful listening and watching for reactions is very important. So the observer helps, passes information to the chief negotiator, and asks for time for a caucus, or private conference, among his team, when he believes that tactical considerations require a rethinking of their position.

Recorder

The third role is that of recorder. This individual is responsible for the maintenance of written records of each of the bargaining sessions. Two sets of records need be kept if the bargaining team is to be well served.

The first set of records will set down the basic facts of each meeting: when the meeting took place, who was present for each side, which issues were discussed, the nature of any agreements reached. Each recorder keeps such information on paper providing a place for a representative of the other team to initial and date to indicate the accuracy of the record. A major purpose of such a record grows from the legal obligation to meet at reasonable times and confer in good faith on the subjects for negotiations. This record, initialed by the other party, is insurance that an unfair-labor-practice charge based on failure to meet this requirement will not be filed at some later date.

The second set of records consists of private notes for the confidential use of the members of one's own bargaining team. In planning how to conduct the next session, which items to press, what concessions may be necessary, and so forth, the team must have more than memory of what went on in past sessions to guide its decisions. A primary source of information for these "our eyes only" records are notes from the observer identifying modifications in wording, hints at possible shifts of position, evidence of possible splits in the ranks of the opposition, or any similar data which can be used to plan for future sessions.

GOOD FAITH AT THE BARGAINING TABLE

Once each side has chosen its representatives, the stage is set for their first meeting across the bargaining table. The language of the Taft-Hartley Act (discussed in Chapter 1), related state statutes, and the traditions of collective bargaining require that each team come to that table committed to bargain in good faith. This requirement has spawned the most litigation, and is subject to more differences of opinion than any other part of the laws of bargaining.

The Taft-Hartley Act, in requiring bargaining to be conducted in good faith, also includes the phrase, "does not compel either party to agree to a proposal or to require the making of a concession." What then, one may ask, is required of negotiators? What is implied when one is required to negotiate in good faith but is not required to agree?

Findings of the National Labor Relations Board have clarified this concept. Where similar laws exist, representatives of the board must meet with representatives of the teacher organization at reasonable times and at mutually agreeable places. Both must come prepared to engage in an honest interchange of views in an attempt to reach understanding and agreement. They are not required to make a final binding agreement, since both sides normally take separate ratification action. But they must be empowered to reach tentative agreements subject to that later ratification.

The Adversary Relationship Is Manifest

The adversary nature of collective bargaining was discussed earlier. At the bargaining table it is manifest in its clearest form. Those who negotiate on behalf of teachers will, and should, put their efforts into securing an agreement most favorable to the interests of the teachers. The requirements of good faith do not require the representative of employees to sublimate the interests of its constituents to any larger consideration. Management representatives are also expected to be vigorous in defending the position of the board of education and administration. They are charged with responsibility for the public interest in operating schools as efficiently and effectively as possible. Nothing in the concept of good faith is meant to require either to forgo the aggressive pursuit of an agreement favorable to the interests of the party each represents.

The Search for Agreement   {CRITERIA OF GOOD FAITH

What both parties are required to do is to try to reach an agreement. Both must put forth efforts to find a basis of mutual consent on which to continue the employer-employee relationship. When agreement eludes them, each has the burden of proof to demonstrate, if required, that everything, short of the exceptions of the law, was done to try to reach an agreement.

Response is a key criterion. Where one party offers a proposal, the other must respond in some way. If the response is acceptance, agreement has been reached. If the proposal is denied, the offering of a counterproposal may help to reach an agreement. At the very least, the party concerned is required to give a full explanation of why it cannot accept the proposal. Presumably, through this process of proposal and response, both sides will come to a clearer understanding of the needs and problems of the other, and an area of possible compromise will emerge.

Willingness to continue to try is another criterion of good faith. If either party breaks off negotiations without the consent of the other, a presumption exists that the mandate of good faith has been broken. The idea is that bargaining may ultimately be successful if the parties continue to work at the problem of seeking a common ground of agreement.

Sharing of information is implied. Documentation of positions by fact demonstrates the honest intent of each party to make its position clear to the other in the hope that clarity will bring possible agreement. Parties to negotiations demonstrate their fidelity to good faith when they bring facts and figures to the bargaining table to buttress their arguments.

Good faith can hardly be extended to forbid human beings, in the press of a conflict situation, from losing tempers or exhibiting very aggressive behavior. Good faith may, however, be put into question if such behavior exceeds reasonable bounds. It may convince an arbitrator that one or the other of the parties to the negotiations has allowed personal or organizational antipathies to interfere with its obligation to seek a mutually acceptable agreement.

Good-faith requirements set up a tightrope for the parties. Each is required to try to reach a voluntary agreement with the other. Both must do what they can to demonstrate a desire to reach that agreement. Neither, however, is required to make any concession. They must both negotiate, but neither is required to surrender.

PROPOSAL AND COUNTEROFFER

Both the everyday concept of bargaining and the requirements of good faith lead the negotiations teams toward a somewhat stylized ritual in bargaining. One side makes an offer. The other side considers it, rejects it as inadequate or unreasonable, and suggests a counterproposal that may partially meet the requirements of the other. The give-and-take progresses, and as it does, both sides cautiously edge toward a middle ground. Bargaining is successful when each finds a position, perhaps less than what it would prefer, but sufficiently acceptable for a tentative agreement to be consummated.

The Settlement Range

Analysis of the bargaining act has led to the development of the concept of a settlement range (see Figure 1). The reasoning goes like this. Each side has a goal in mind. This position on an issue is what they would establish if they could unilaterally decide the issue. This goal is revealed to their adversary early in bargaining. Normally it will be the initial offer each makes.

Each side also has a resistance point. That means the place on each issue where a party to negotiations would prefer to break off negotiations rather than make a further concession. This is the point where disagreement is preferred to agreement on any less desirable terms. In the case, for instance, of a proposal by a teacher organization for increased salaries for beginning teachers, the goal might be a figure of $10,000. But the organization may well realize that the present financial circumstances and beliefs held by the board of education make that goal unlikely. So the organization calculates as best it can what might be achieved and what its membership would be willing to accept. If that were $8,500, then that figure would be the resistance point, the point at which the organization would refuse to accept a lower figure almost regardless of the consequences. In this hypothetical situation, suppose the board has determined that its budget would provide for an increase to $7,500 without difficulty and has that as its goal. The board may also determine that if pressed, it could go as high as $9,000, although it prefers not to commit so large a portion of its funds to salaries. Thus, a goal and a resistance point exist for each party. One can see that a zone of potential agreement exists, ranging from $8,500, the lowest figure the teacher organization would accept, to $9,000, the highest figure the board would offer. Potential agreement can be reached anywhere be-

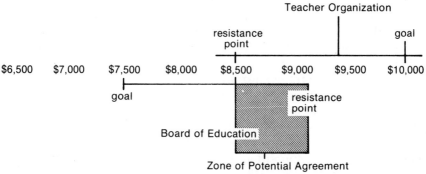

Figure 1. Zone of Potential Agreement

tween these points. The task of the negotiator is to find a point within this zone that is as close as possible to the goal of his constituents and to get agreement at that point.

This discussion makes these determinations appear simple. Actually, great difficulty is often encountered by the negotiators. This is especially true in the case of those who represent teachers or other employee groups. Consensus on goals is difficult enough. At best it represents a middle-ground opinion of the membership. How the negotiator is to judge an appropriate resistance point is much more difficult. The question is, at what point would a substantial majority of the membership prefer to accept the alternatives to agreement—working without an agreement, a strike or other job action—to having the matter settled? Informal discussion with key leaders in the various subsections of the organization is an important testing ground. Membership meetings at which open discussion of concerns can be voiced also help. The problem is exacerbated by the fact that feelings on such questions are fluid, rather than fixed. An accurate reading of the desired resistance point of the membership at the beginning of negotiations may become inaccurate due to intervening happenings which either inflame passions and increase militancy or lead to an increased desire for a settlement even at a lower figure than was once felt to be minimal.

The same problem is faced by those representing management. However, their immediate constituency, the board of education, is a much smaller group, and consequently communication and thus the development of a common point of view is somewhat easier.

Tactical Considerations

The goal is communicated to the opposition in the early stages of negotiations. The resistance point of each side is initially a carefully guarded secret. The leakage of the minimum one would accept, or the maximum one would be willing to grant, guarantees that nothing else will be accepted by one's adversary. So negotiators must keep the true resistance point secret even from their own constituents. This further compounds the difficulty of the negotiator, who must judge the resistance point acceptable to his client, but cannot tell his client what it is that he has in mind since that increases the possibility of a leak.

As negotiations progress, negotiators attempt to suggest false resistance points to the opposition. If one can persuade his opponent that one is unable to retreat further, one forces him to settle at that point or accept a breakdown in negotiations. Thus, in the example, the teacher negotiator may say, "Anything less than $9,000 would greatly

damage our chances of ratification. Teachers would be very unhappy."
In this way he attempts to suggest, without actually saying so, that the
resistance point of the teacher organization is $9,000 when actually it
is $8,500. That figure, it so happens, is within the zone of potential
agreement, and if the opponent believes that this is the actual resistance point, an agreement will probably be consummated at that figure
—which is above the minimum acceptable to the teachers, and hence
very successful negotiations for them.

These tactics must be carefully thought out. The danger is that a
negotiator may commit himself to a given resistance point—"That's the
lowest we would be willing to go"—when, in fact, he would be willing
and able to go lower. If this point is outside the zone of potential
agreement, an impasse will be created. Now that negotiator is in a
difficult position. One choice is to "tough it out." This is disadvantageous
since he may force a strike which he knows his own membership will
not support. The other choice is equally unpleasant. It is awkward to
inform one's opponent that one really didn't mean it, and would be
willing to continue to negotiate toward a lower figure. That admission
destroys credibility, and future statements that one cannot accept less
may not be believed either.

The Necessary Ritual

Collective negotiations are frequently culminated in wearing, last-
minute, round-the-clock sessions during which both sides make concessions they were unwilling to make earlier. Most of us have seen news
photographs of bleary-eyed bargainers announcing an agreement
which stayed off a strike and relieved the public of potential discomfi-
ture if not serious hardship. Why these dramatics? Why can't negotiations be conducted in a more businesslike fashion?

Part of the answer to this lies in pressures that are felt by both
negotiation teams. Each has been sent to the table to get an agreement
its constituency desires. Each faces the necessity of achieving ratification of the agreement by those whom they represent. Any agreement,
in all likelihood, will fall short of the hopes of the constituency. So the
negotiators face the problem of persuading those who sent them that
the agreement they bring back is the best that could have been
achieved. If the agreement is consummated quickly, it may appear that
further concessions might have been won if the negotiators had per-
sisted. Further, both negotiators realize that there is truth in this. Who
knows what concessions might be won by the side that appears ready
to let the time run out rather than give any more? Each negotiator can

test the other's resolve and actual resistance point by a form of brink-manship with the contract deadline.

A second, related aspect bears consideration. The members of the union and the board of education alike will have indicated their goals to their negotiators prior to the onset of negotiations. Both teams will probably realize early that those goals will only be partially reached. However, the negotiators are not likely to get ratification until their constituents realize that the goals will be only partially achieved, and that the balance-of-power nature of the bargaining relationship requires considerable accommodation to the demands of the other side. As negotiations run their course and time passes with little apparent progress, the first hot blush of anticipation of a bright future is replaced by a growing acceptance that half-a-loaf is probably as much as one may expect to receive. This takes time. An agreement completed too early might fail of ratification because sufficient time for disillusionment to set in has not transpired.

These thoughts should not be taken as an argument that all of bargaining is an act played out for the benefit of manipulated constituents. Time is necessary for the hard work of analyzing demands, costing out proposals, and seeking possible alternatives that can meet the needs of one party without damaging the essential requirements of the other. The hard give-and-take of proposal-counterproposal helps each side to understand the problems and priorities of the other. With this understanding often comes the insight necessary to develop creative compromise.

Quid Pro Quo

Quid pro quo is a concept closely connected with bargaining, and the fact that it is stated in Latin ought not lead the reader to believe that there is anything obscure about it. Most people intuitively understand that the bargaining act involves a trading of items of value in order to receive other things which are desired even more. At the market, the buyer trades cash for goods, and the merchant trades goods for cash. Each gives up something of value in order to receive something which serves his immediate purposes more adequately.

When the bargaining teams confront each other across the table, much the same kind of transaction must take place if agreement is to be consummated. Each has priorities and needs. Each is somewhat under the control of the other to the extent that the satisfaction of these desires can only come through the action of the other. Each has a sense of price in mind; a judgment of the relative worth of what is sought both to the one who seeks and to the one who has.

While this may seem self-evident, it is not infrequent that inexperienced negotiators forget this simple concept. Even more frequently, those they represent forget it. When a teacher-organization bargaining team goes to the table, they will try to achieve what the membership desires. The membership needs to keep in mind that this agreement normally will come at some cost. Before the representatives of management will agree to a proposal, they must achieve something of benefit to management. By the same token, management may have some proposals which it would like adopted. Where this is the case, concessions may reasonably be sought as the price of agreement.

Currency for this transaction is frequently a problem. Normally, teacher organizations are attempting to bring about change. Normally, management representatives are attempting to reduce the demands of teachers to a point they believe to be reasonable. Part of the currency is the desire of management to have the proposals reduced, either by removing some of them from the list of demands, or by reducing the extent of those which are insisted upon. Negotiators for teachers can "buy" agreements by "spending" some of the total goals of their organization. Administration representatives can "buy" reductions in demands by "spending" resources of time or money. One can engage in this kind of transaction better when one has an understanding of the values and priorities of the other side. The clearer the understanding, the more one can judge how much to expect for each concession.

In the lexicon of negotiations, these transactions are termed *movement*. One side "moves" by reducing its demand, thus coming closer to the position of the other. Negotiators are careful not to make two successive movements. Once a movement is consummated, negotiators wait for an acceptable countermovement, or exchange of currency, from the other side. Thus, in negotiations the responsibility for acting shifts from side to side. Each tries to take action in such a way as to suggest "real movement" without going further than necessary. Judging whether a restatement of a position is nothing more than saying the same thing in new words or is actually a substantive concession is an important part of negotiations.

It is important for teachers to remember that their representatives will have to reduce demands in order to wring concessions from the representatives of the board of education. Sometimes members will say, "We ought not ask for anything more than we deserve, and we ought not accept anything less than our full requirements." This rhetoric is apt to bring vocal support at a membership meeting. It creates hardships for those who are to represent teachers in negotiations, however. The essence of bargaining is the quid pro quo—the give-and-take toward compromise. Inflexible positions stated in moralistic terms can hardly be modified without suggesting absence of commitment. The negotiators for teacher organizations will have difficulty enough in serving the interests of teachers without being faced with a charge of "sell-out" whenever they make necessary reductions in demands in order to achieve agreement.

The Impact of Politics

It would be simplistic to assume that the establishment of resistance points and goals by the two parties is done in isolation from the rest of the world. Both the teacher bargaining agent and the board of education are influenced in decision-making by their expectations of public support or opposition. Forces from the general political sphere may be felt throughout the bargaining process.

Boards of education, as public representatives, are required to conduct the public business in accordance with the public will. If they ignore or misread public opinion in coming to agreements with teacher representatives, action designed to undo those agreements will be brought into play. This may mean defeat of tax-levy proposals needed to fund the agreement, or replacement of the incumbents at the next board election.

Teacher organizations are not directly responsible to the public. Their responsibility is to their membership. Nevertheless, since the membership is a part of the public, and since public support or opposition influences membership opinion, an indirect impact occurs. Further, teacher organizations that are part of, or allied with, the broader labor movement must consider its opinion. An AFT local, for instance, may belong to a local council of labor unions. Part of the strength of the AFT local derives from this affiliation and the implied supportive strength of labor in general. In some communities, the opinion of labor and public opinion may be virtually identical. In any case, the opinion of organized labor is a weighty factor. So teacher organizations need and seek general public support.

As both parties determine their positions for bargaining, they do so keeping one eye upon anticipated public reaction. Other political forces in the community are potential allies or hindrances. A statement by the mayor, a resolution by the municipal council, the opinions of community-based organizations, editorial and news coverage by the media, and the judgment of the shadowy power structure of the community all influence public opinion. So what is to be demanded by teacher groups, and what is to be resisted by the board, is determined in the context of political considerations. Further, once the parties begin to bargain, reconsideration of resistance points often results from a continuing assessment of the political climate. Neither can ignore it, except at its own peril.

INTRAORGANIZATIONAL BARGAINING

Bargaining between the protagonists across the bargaining table is the most observable part of the process. This should not lead one to disregard the importance and intensity of negotiations within the ranks of each side. Earlier, mention was made of the use of a single spokesman at the table in order to confront the adversary with the appearance of unity. Interaction to determine the position the negotiator will take requires considerable and sometimes emotion-laden bargaining. Neither the board of education nor the teachers' organization is a monolith. Each will have majority, minority, and undecided opinions on virtually any issue. Debate designed to accommodate these differences is termed intraorganizational bargaining.

Strains on Teacher Organizations

Some typical sources of difference can be anticipated within the teacher bargaining agent. Elementary teachers may differ from secondary teachers on issues of preparation time. Older teachers may be more concerned with accumulation of sick leave than younger ones. Those who have taught for a number of years are likely to be more interested in salary maximums than increments at the lower end of the scale. Teachers with families may prefer more insurance to other benefits. And so it goes. The leadership of the organization must develop bargaining positions and then determine compromises and counterproposals during bargaining in such a way as to retain the support of the various factions. Failure to do so may threaten necessary ratification of the agreement once it is consummated. Disappointed factions may seek to overthrow the leadership of the organization.

While all will agree that it is necessary to mask the differences within the ranks in order to strengthen bargaining positions, this is frequently difficult to accomplish. Sharp differences of opinion within the executive committee of the teachers' organization may be related to attempts to replace the leadership. These considerations may tempt some to leak information to the membership at large in hopes of weakening the strength of incumbents. Once information is widely discussed, the negotiators for the board of education are sure to become aware of it.

Strains on Management

Those who represent administration are subject to the same necessity to work out agreement within their ranks in order to be able to negotiate with teachers. Administrators may well have different priorities from members of the board of education. Within the board, differences of opinion are likely. The chief negotiator must seek compromise of these differences in order to be able to communicate a position at the table.

Board members face difficult problems. They are public representatives with obligations to their constituents. It is often awkward for them to refuse comment to questions from citizens, or to appear to support a position with which they disagree in order to preserve the bargaining position of the board. Yet failure to accomplish this delicate task is very harmful to the chief negotiator who represents them.

Problems of the Chief Negotiator

Difficult intraorganizational bargaining takes place in caucus sessions during the actual face-to-face negotiations. A compromise offer by the adversary normally results in the negotiation team's retiring to a private room for a short time in order to decide what to do next. Should the compromise be accepted? Should another counteroffer be presented which moves in that direction but is more favorable to one's own interest? Should the matter be delayed until the next bargaining session in order to give time for consultation with the party one represents? Or, is the atmosphere favorable now and should the opportunity be grasped? These and related tactical decisions must be made, relatively quickly, under considerable tension, and often late at night, by bargaining teams that have already spent much of their energy and patience. One expects dispute from the adversary across the bargaining table. Argument from one's colleagues in the caucus session is harder to take. Emotions surface quickly in such situations. Yet the necessity for returning with a position to which all on the bargaining team can subscribe is pressing.

RATIFICATION

A collectively bargained agreement between the representatives of the teachers and those representing the board of education is of no consequence until it has been transformed into official board-of-education policy. Policy can only be established by the board, in regular public session, upon formal motion and affirmative vote. Where the motion is to accept the agreement hammered out through negotiations, this process is called ratification.

Teacher organizations commonly also ratify the agreement reached by negotiators through a vote of the membership of the association or union. This, however, is not always the case. How the union chooses to operate is a matter for it to decide through its own constitution and by-laws. If, however, its constitution requires ratification, courts will require that the union abide by its own procedures.

Protection for the Parties

The advantages of a ratification process are, perhaps, self-evident. The agreement will be between the teachers' organization and the board of education as the principal parties. However, neither of them has participated directly in the negotiation of that agreement. Both have been represented by those they trusted to carry out their purposes. Without delayed ratification, it would not be possible to negate errors made by these representatives.

Ratification takes place several days after the final initialing of the tentative agreements. This period of time makes it possible for each side to have attorneys check the wording of the agreements for possible legal implications of which the negotiators may have been unaware. Of even greater importance, it makes it possible for a second look to be taken by all who are to be affected by the agreement.

Collective negotiation seeks voluntary agreement. Without ratification, one could not be confident that the document represents the freely given consent of the parties to the agreement.

A Shift in Role for the Chief Negotiator

Consider the task of the chief negotiator again for a moment. He, and the others on the negotiation team, was sent to the table to try to achieve, insofar as possible, the goals of the party being represented. He assessed, as best as possible, the extent to which those being represented would be willing to accept half-a-loaf as the price of agreement. But no guarantees were ever possible.

The task of the negotiator is to achieve agreement with the other party in light of these goals. If he achieves agreement at the table, and then has that agreement rejected by those he represents, he has failed.

Almost certainly he will have to be replaced. Achieving ratification of the tentative agreement is absolutely necessary.

The negotiator returns to those who sent him with an agreement short of what they had hoped for. Now he must argue the desirability of accepting this agreement, which reflects the accomplishment of some of the aims of the opposing group. So a chief negotiator for the board of education, for instance, argues the wisdom of accepting aspects of the agreement that had been advocated by teacher representatives. He finds himself making the arguments to the board that his opponent has just recently been making to him. The chief negotiator for the teacher organization, similarly, attempts to explain to the membership why certain clauses in the agreement favorable to the interests of the board are reasonable and should be agreed to.

Experienced negotiators develop an unspoken but very real understanding of the task each will face in arguing for ratification at the conclusion of negotiations. Each realizes that his self-interest, as well as the interest of those he represents, is served by the success of his adversary in presenting the agreement for ratification. Wise negotiators work with and through each other to do what they can to insure that their counterpart has no undue difficulty in achieving ratification.

SUMMARY

The collective-bargaining process includes a series of interactions, which take place in an overlapping fashion. The diagram in Figure 2 attempts to show these relationships. It is possible to identify five partially distinct areas. Only one of these involves direct contact between the parties to negotiations. The other four represent meetings which must take place among the members of each side in planning and conducting the negotiations process.

Areas 1 and 1(a) represent contact between the negotiators and the principals they represent. Minimum goals and minimum-acceptance understandings are agreed to initially, reviewed while negotiations are in process, and finally ratified in these discussions.

Areas 2 and 2(a) represent the sites of tactical planning. The negotiating teams meet here with the leaders of those they represent. The positioning of preliminary offers, responses to offers of the other party, tentative resolution subject to final ratification, and decisions for accommodation or continued resistance are made here.

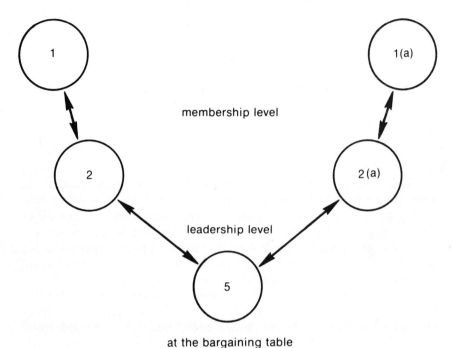

at the bargaining table

Figure 2. The Interactions of Collective Bargaining

The fifth circle encompasses the arena in which the representatives of both adversaries meet, advance proposals as planned, receive responses, engage in communication and in appraisal of the movements of the opposition. This is where the drama is played out. Decisions that may lead to agreement are communicated here. It is often not the place where the decisions are made.

CHAPTER 4

Impasse

The process discussed in the previous chapter may result in an agreement into which each party enters voluntarily. When that happens, a promising basis for continued operation of the schools exists. During the time span of the agreement, both the employing board and the employed teachers work together according to terms each has agreed are acceptable. Both have chosen agreement on these terms rather than disagreement with its attendant uncertainies.

Collective negotiations do not guarantee this desirable result; negotiations only make it possible. As has been discussed, the settlement may be impossible because the minimum acceptable terms of each party may not overlap. Political pressures may bring about a refusal to ratify a tentative agreement. The negotiators may inadvertently find themselves in positions where the necessary retreat in order to achieve compromise may be impossible due to misunderstandings or concern for face-saving. These and other possibilities require exploration of the consequences of impasse; the persisting failure of the negotiators to reach agreement. This chapter will discuss several alternatives which have been used, or proposed, as means by which an agreement can be consummated in spite of failure of the two parties to reach agreement in their deliberations at the bargaining table.

Some impasse procedures are attempts to assist the parties themselves to find the agreement which has eluded them. Others are imposed settlements decided by a third party and imposed through coercion. Consideration of the relative merits of the various proposals ought to be undertaken with one principle in mind. When both parties agree voluntarily, both are more likely to try to make the agreement work out in day-to-day practice. Difficulties will certainly arise. Where the parties have freely determined that the agreement is acceptable, each has a stake in resolving difficulties within the framework of that agreement.

Where settlements have been imposed on one or perhaps both of the parties through coercion, a different attitude is predictable. If one party feels the agreement is unfair and is on record as opposing it as unworkable, that party is unlikely to feel a commitment to ensuring the success of the settlement. More likely a self-fulfilling prophecy may be instituted so that the predictions of unworkability by one side or the other become accurate. At the very least, an imposed settlement which is viewed by one side as a defeat, sets in motion forces planning toward the next round of negotiations as the theater for revanchism.

In the earliest days of collective bargaining in industry, only one result of failure at the bargaining table could be anticipated. "No contract no work" was the battle cry of militant unionists. The strike was the only recourse of disappointed workers. Production requirements during World War II necessitated the development of alternate responses to failure at the bargaining table. Even after the war, the impact of work stoppages, in many cases, was such a heavy blow to the national economy, or promised so much public suffering, that the necessity for strike avoidance became more widely accepted. Unions, as well as management, have oftimes found that the costs of strikes outweighted gains from the eventual settlement. Both employee organizations and management have been willing to explore alternative means of resolving impasses at the bargaining table.

In public employment, strikes have, for the most part, been prohibited. The belief that strikes in public employment are tantamount to the use of force against the public, stemming from the Boston police strike of 1919, has been codified into law. In the few jurisdictions where strikes in public employment are permitted, legal and moral pressure for strike-avoiding processes is strong. This is not to say that strikes have not been called in public employment, both in conformity with and in defiance of the law. But much interest in avoiding strikes exists, and the search for alternative responses to impasse continues.

MEDIATION

Mediation is an attempt to bridge the gap between the two parties that has resulted in a breakdown of negotiations. First, it assumes that the two parties still wish to reach agreement, but are having difficulty in doing so. Secondly, it assumes that an outside party can interact with both in such a way as to secure their confidence and thus be able to provide counsel to each.

Mediation normally begins with the appointment or joint selection of an individual to serve as mediator. Where laws require mediation, the parties to bargaining must inform some agency, normally a state employment board, that an impasse exists. The state agency then appoints a mediator to work with the parties. In the absence of legal requirements, the two parties themselves may agree to seek the assistance of a mediator. They may simply agree on someone acceptable to both and jointly request that person's services. Or they may agree to utilize the services of the American Arbitration Association. This association is a widely respected private agency, which, among other services, provides trained neutral experts who can assist in the resolution of impasses.

The mediator usually meets independently with each party. He hopes that each will accept his neutrality and integrity to the degree that each will reveal to him the minimum acceptable settlement position on the issues in dispute. If this takes place, he may be able to see what is masked from the parties themselves. He may discover a potential basis for agreement. If so, the mediator is in a position to discuss the potential basis separately with the protagonists. The hope is that such discussion will enable them to return to the bargaining table and come to a voluntary agreement. In a sense, the role of the mediator is like that of a marriage counselor. Only the two parties themselves can establish the basis for their continued living and working in conjunction with each other. But the perceptive third party may be able to help them reach that agreement.

Advantages of the Mediation Process

The biggest advantage of the mediation process is the voluntary nature of the resulting agreement. Neither of the parties commits more than it feels just or acceptable. Both have merely been assisted to do what they wanted to do anyway. So the agreement is launched with the maximum possibility of successful implementation.

The mediation process is relatively inexpensive. While the time of the mediator may not be all that inexpensive, relatively little time may be required, at least in comparison with other impasse-resolution devices.

The win-loss syndrome is avoided. The mediator may be able to assist this by serving as a scapegoat. Sometimes an impasse has resulted from one party having negotiated itself into a position where any further retreat would appear, both to the other side and perhaps to its own constituency, to be a surrender. One or both negotiators may find it politically possible to "cooperate with the negotiator" and accept his proposal, even though acceptance of the same proposal, if it were put forward by the adversary, would be damaging. In that case, face-saving permits the two parties to agree and to secure ratification, which otherwise might have been blocked.

Problems with Mediation

Trustful, open communication between each of the parties and the neutral mediator may not be so readily achievable as one would hope. If either party views the mediator as an ally of the other, bent upon winning for the other what they could not win for themselves, mediation is impossible.

Where the mediator comes on assignment from a state board, this is particularly apt to be a difficulty. Who knows what instructions this stranger with a briefcase brings from the state capital? Who knows what hidden agenda may lie behind his actions? Employee groups, particularly, are apt to be suspicious of his neutrality, particularly if state political figures have expressed any opinions contrary to their objectives.

The joint selection of someone known and trusted by both sides avoids this difficulty. However, this individual may not be knowledgeable about the process of collective bargaining or of the intricacies of the issues in dispute. In that case, even after full disclosure by the parties, he may find it impossible to exercise the insight necessary to the development of a creative proposal for solution. Issues at impasse are, inevitably, thorny and involved. Their resolution requires more than good intentions.

ADVISORY ARBITRATION

Two terms, *fact finding* and *advisory arbitration,* are used to describe what is essentially the same process. Sometimes discussion includes the term *fact finding with recommendation.* No substantive distinction exists between any of these terms. Advisory arbitration can be used following mediation in cases where mediation has not resulted in resolution. Nothing in the two processes requires the parties to choose between them.

Like mediation, advisory arbitration may be required by law in jurisdictions where bargaining is mandated. In such cases, the law prescribes the process as a means of arriving at an agreement when the collective-bargaining process unaided has failed. Also like mediation, advisory arbitration attempts to create a situation wherein the two parties will voluntarily consent and ratify the basis for continued employment relations.

Arbitration may be performed by a single arbitrator or by an arbitration panel. Where a panel is used, a frequent convention is for each side to select a person in whom it has confidence, and for these two persons to select another who will serve as chairman of the panel and bear the primary responsibility for conducting the arbitration action.

A formal hearing will be arranged. Both sides to the dispute will be invited to be present and to provide such fact and argumentation as each desires to demonstrate the justice or appropriateness of its position on each of the issues in dispute. The hearing is conducted in an orderly fashion, with each side given an opportunity to present its case without interruption. Each is given an opportunity to rebut the testimony of the other. While this has the general appearance of a courtroom proceeding, it is less formal than that. Arbitrators may be lawyers, and counsel may present evidence at the hearing, but it is not usually necessary to observe the formal rules of evidence.

Arbitrators often give wide latitude to each party in the presentation of its case in order to find facts or circumstances needed to reach a conclusion.

After the hearing, the arbitrator, or the arbitration panel, will take into consideration the facts and arguments presented by each side and reach a conclusion believed to be a fair basis upon which the parties could agree. This conclusion is then transmitted to each side. Frequently, it is understood that the recommendations for settlement will first be given privately to the two parties. After a given period of time, if they have not agreed, the recommendations may be made public.

Advantages of Advisory Arbitration

This process, like mediation, leaves the final determination of the agreement to the voluntary acceptance of the two parties to the dispute. To be sure, the nature of that agreement has reflected the opinion of a third force, but acceptance or rejection remains with those who must put the agreement into effect. The factor of consent, of such great value in the concept of negotiations, is preserved.

Arbitration is not so dependent upon the ability of a third party to gain the trust of the parties. Unlike mediation, no private exchange of confidence is necessary. The recommendation of the arbitrator will be accompanied by the reasoning behind his advice. Each party can evaluate that reasoning independently of their feelings about the arbitrator or the panel.

A form of pressure is implicit in the potential for public disclosure. Where the impasse is hardened, something may be needed to tip the scales toward preference for agreement on given terms rather than preference for continued disagreement.

Public opinion is a matter of concern to both the board of education and teacher organizations. Obstinancy in the privacy of the bargaining room is easier for both than a public posture of unreasonableness. Where each knows that the public will be aware of the compromise proposal from a neutral party, each is under some compulsion to accept it rather than face the possible consequences of disclosure as the one refusing to compromise.

Arbitration is reasonably expensive. The time of the arbitrators, the representatives of the two disputants, attorneys, and stenographers all contribute to the substantial cost of conducting the hearing. These costs, normally, are shared equally by the teacher organization and the board of education. This factor may impel the two parties to agree at the bargaining table rather than incur expenses only to get a recommendation they might just as well have developed on their own.

Problems with Advisory Arbitration

The major problem with advisory arbitration is the dilution of consent. To be sure, both parties are free to accept or reject the advice of the panel. However, the settlement, if one emerges, is not the product of the initiative of those who will put the agreement into operation. Less motivation to make it work exists than is the case where negotiation has produced the compromise.

In advisory arbitration, as well as in other forms of arbitration to be discussed later, tactical considerations may well diminish the chances for negotiations to be successful. The reason for this is the natural tendency of each side to "save something for the arbitrator." Where the parties anticipate arbitration, they must assume that the recommendation of the arbitrator will require a compromise between the final positions offered by each. This is not necessarily always the case, but prudence requires that assumption. If that is anticipated, both parties must position their last offer to the other at a point short of their actual minimum acceptable position. This establishes a resistance point during negotiations short of the actual minimum acceptable position. This action by both sides serves to shrink the zone of potential agreement markedly, if not to obliterate it. Thus agreement at the table is made less likely, or even blocked, by the anticipation of arbitration.

A third problem of arbitration is an even greater threat to successful negotiations. The two parties may come together with the attitude that these negotiations are merely a formality preceding the submission of differences to arbitration. The good-faith effort to reach agreement at the table, which is the sparkplug of the negotiations process, is absent. In the absence of effort to agree, the narrowing of the dispute and the growth in understanding of the priorities and needs of one's adversary, which often provide the foundation for acceptance of the compromise of the arbitrator, is omitted. Failure of good-faith bargaining subverts the advisory arbitration process as well.

VOLUNTARY BINDING ARBITRATION

Both sides, teacher organization and board of education, may, if they wish, agree to submit those issues upon which they fail to agree to arbitration in a process quite like that just described. The distinction is that this agreement may include the understanding that both will abide by the recommendation and ratify it. The distinction should be made clear. In advisory arbitration, the two parties take the settlement recommended by the arbitrator back for ratification in the same manner that agreements hammered out at the bargaining table are submitted for ratification. In voluntary binding arbitration, both sides commit themselves to ratification of any agreement determined by the arbitrator *prior* to knowing what that agreement may be.

Advantages of Voluntary Binding Arbitration

Some measure of consent remains, although it clearly is much diluted. The two parties do not consent to specific terms. They merely have consented to a process by which the terms of their continued employment relationship are to be determined.

The primary advantage of voluntary binding arbitration is that it greatly insures against strikes. Both mediation and advisory arbitration preserve the freedom of both parties to continue to disagree. That continuation may well result in a strike. Strikes are, or can be, costly to teachers as well as to the public. These high potential costs threaten both teacher organizations and boards. Both may value insurance against strikes.

But they may not. Teachers may feel that the ultimate threat of a strike is the source of their bargaining power. They may fear that a commitment to accept arbitration may lead school boards to reason that there is little to fear from failure to agree. Boards may secretly value potential strikes. They may reason that needed revenue increases may be thus brought about.

A potential for taxation without representation is a problem with voluntary binding arbitration in public employment. All agreements require funds to implement them. Funds, in the case of public education, come largely from shifting present allocations or from increased taxation. Boards of education are the only agencies legally authorized to make such decisions. Where the decision is shifted to an arbitrator, a person unaccountable to the public makes a decision that will determine the extent of taxation of that public as well as the allocation of public funds. As will be discussed in the next chapter, voluntary binding arbitration has been widely used to settle disputes about what an agreement stipulates. But this is quite different from decisions about what the agreement *shall be*.

COMPULSORY BINDING ARBITRATION

Proposals have been made that legislatures supplement requirements for collective bargaining with further legislation requiring boards of education and those representing employees to submit disputes that cannot be resolved through collective bargaining to the binding arbitration process described above. The distinction is that there would be no freedom to decide whether or not to do. Legislation of this sort is rare in the United States, although similar laws are in existence in other countries. Widespread implementation of such legislation would presumably require the creation of a system of what might be termed labor courts for public employment disputes.

Advantages Claimed for Compulsory Binding Arbitration

Since there has been little actual experience with compulsory binding arbitration, only the intent of such legislation can be assessed. Supporters argue that collective bargaining would be enhanced, since failure to agree would expose the parties to the uncertainties of an imposed agreement from which recourse is impossible.

The primary purpose of compulsory binding arbitration is the avoidance of strikes. An analogue may be advanced. Disputes over fulfillment of contracts, performance of obligations, or damages inflicted upon others are settled through the courts, at least in part because this frees the public from the strife attendant upon private settlement of disputes. Similarly, disputes over employment circumstances would also have an established, sanctioned, neutral system of courts to determine equity so that the public does not become the innocent victim of a failure of bargaining.

Problems with Compulsory Binding Arbitration

The voluntary nature of agreements on employment relations disappears altogether with compulsory binding arbitration. If bargaining fails, a settlement fixing questions of wages, hours, and terms and conditions of employment is imposed upon the parties. Governmental intervention in attempting to control wages and prices has had a spotty history in our country. Whether Americans would be willing to submit to governmental fiat as the determiner of wages, especially when this only applied to those in public employment, or whether this is alien to the concept of free men in a free economy, can only be speculated upon. It is even more questionable whether an imposed settlement, believed to be unfair by one or both parties, could result in productive enterprise.

LAST-BEST-OFFER ARBITRATION

An inventive proposal has been advanced which seeks to reverse the tendency for all forms of arbitration to interfere with the process of collective negotiations. This proposal attempts to harness tactical considerations of self-interest to the achievement of voluntary settlements. At the same time, its proponents claim that it is at least as sound as process for the resolution of impasse without strikes as any other forms of arbitration. Because of the nature of this proposal, it is often referred to as the "last-best-offer" form of arbitration. This is how it works.

Negotiations proceed between the two parties as is now the case. Good-faith bargaining will, it is hoped, provide a basis for agreement. Upon the declaration of an impasse by one or both of the parties, an arbitrator is selected or appointed similarly to the process of advisory arbitration discussed earlier. In this instance, however, the arbitrator performs a task different in one important respect. The sole option open to the arbitrator is to choose between two alternative possibilities: the last best offer made by the representative of the employees and the last best offer made by the employer's agent. The arbitrator is forbidden to compromise or to make an award that varies in any way from one of the two final proposals.

Presumably, the arbitrator would consider the two alternative offers in comparison with similar settlements and going wages, similar tax-base and enrollment figures, and such other determinants of a fair settlement which he or she believed appropriate. In light of these considerations, one or the other of the last best offers would be the one both parties would be required to accept.

Advantages Claimed for Last-Best-Offer Arbitration

Proponents of this approach argue that both parties naturally seek tactical advantages in planning their bargaining offers. Each party would wish to position itself so that the arbitrator would choose its offer over that ot its adversary. Since both would be impelled in this direction, both would seek to make a final offer to the other party that would appear to an outsider to be more fair and reasonable than that of the other. Consequently, each would, insofar as possible, try to "top" the last offer of its adversary with a more reasonable basis for settlement. What more, they ask, could a proponent of voluntary collective negotiations desire than an impasse technique which has potential rewards for each party for generosity in proposals at the bargaining table? The natural result, they claim, is that arbitration would only rarely be utilized since the two parties would be virtually assured of reaching an acceptable agreement as a result of their competition in reasonableness.

Problems with Last-Best-Offer Arbitration

Once last-best-offer arbitration is required, proponents predict, it would rarely if ever be used. If it were rarely if ever used, the question of problems of implementation would, of course, be inconsequential. If, on the other hand, actual practice resulted in its use, Potential difficulties would become more of a concern.

The most grievous of the potential disadvantages is the degree to which this process would exacerbate the victory and defeat situations. One offer must be accepted without modification. One must be totally rejected. Thus, one party is forced to live under an agreement resulting from total rejection of its best effort at reaching agreement. Collective negotiation assumes that the work relationship will go smoother as a result of an agreement voluntarily entered into by both parties. Last-best-offer arbitration may result in the opposite, an agreement which one or the other is naturally tempted to sabotage.

The position of the arbitrator appears to be more difficult under this form of arbitration. The interest of the arbitrator under conventional arbitration forms is to find a settlement to recommend which is as acceptable as possible to both parties. To some extent, his continued success and continued utilization in an arbitration role depend upon the extent to which both employee groups and employers believe that he is fair and reasonable. Success at creative compromise is his stock in trade. Under last-best-offer arbitration, one side will inevitably feel that the arbitrator has been unfair in his decision to choose the offer of the other. Each decision, since it requires him to choose one or the other side, renders him suspect as a neutral in future disputes. Thus, in order to continue to serve as an arbitrator, a pattern of choices in which a balance of decisions for and against both parties would be necessary. That balance might come about naturally, but one would have to speculate about the temptation to "even up" if an arbitrator had had a succession of decisions in one or the other direction. An arbitration scheme which has a possibility for the self-interest of the arbitrator to push in directions away from a just settlement is clearly suspect.

SUMMARY

Since collective negotiations cannot guarantee the settling of disputes over wages, hours, and conditions of employment, something is needed in the event of impasse. Strikes, overt efforts to force compliance on the public employer, are forbidden in most jurisdictions and may be growing in unpopularity in all. A search continues to find effective institutionalized means of resolving impasse at the bargaining table without the trauma of a strike.

Mediation and advisory arbitration are techniques drawn from private employment experience that are applicable to public employment needs. Other mechanisms are being sought. Voluntary binding arbitration, compulsory binding arbitration, and last-best-offer arbitration have been proposed as additions to the arsenal of weapons available to those who seek resolution of impasses in bargaining. The search continues for yet more promising techniques.

CHAPTER 5

Teaching under a Negotiated Agreement

Negotiating an employment agreement is different from negotiating a price for a used car. An agreement to buy and sell may be a onetime transaction. When it is closed, each party goes his separate way. An employment agreement is, of course, quite the opposite. The conclusion of the negotiations is not the end, but rather the beginning of a new phase of the continuing relationship. Both parties to the agreement work together daily. The nature of their relationship will have important consequences for the success of the organization and for the happiness of the employees.

Bargaining is somewhat like courtship in that both parties make promises to the other about the way they will behave. The long-term living together of the marriage, with its inevitable conflicts and necessary accommodations, follows.

This chapter examines some of the problems of the continuing employment relationship under the terms of the agreement reached at the bargaining table. Each party to the agreement has obligations to the other as a result of the agreement. Each has the right to expect certain things from the other. A collectively bargained agreement creates circumstances different in important ways from what many were used to prior to collective bargaining. Understanding the changes and the reasons for the changes is important.

DIFFERENCES IN EMPLOYMENT RELATIONSHIPS

Those teaching under a negotiated agreement for the first time may become aware of differences in their relations with administrators. It may not be apparent, however, why the changes have come about. Teachers considering the adoption of collective bargaining need to understand the concomitant changes which are likely.

The Collective Nature of the Agreement

In Chapter 2 the criteria for establishment of a bargaining unit were discussed. Community of interest is one criterion. Because an agreement is binding upon a group of employees, it is necessary that the group be as nearly alike as possible in their employment relationships. Once the agreement is ratified, the importance of this consideration is manifest. All who are in the bargaining unit are to be treated alike. Their treatment is stipulated in the negotiated agreement.

Teachers may find this different from what they have been used to or what they prefer. In teaching, most recognize and use the concept of individual differences. Because no two pupils are exactly alike, the teacher's treatment of students differs. In the same fashion, teachers may have expected to receive individualized consideration of their problems by the administration of the school. In the past, a teacher with a real need was sometimes permitted to leave school early or come in late, or was excused from an obligation. A school that treated all alike according to a fixed set of rules often appeared bureaucratic and lacking in humanism.

Difference in treatment is precisely what collective bargaining seeks to destroy, however. Difference in treatment has sometimes been an expression of favoritism. Administration may have permitted actions from some teachers that were forbidden to others who were less well connected. A keystone of collective bargaining is equal treatment for all under the terms of the contract. Accommodation, or individualized consideration of special needs, is frowned upon and may constitute violation of the agreement.

In a large bargaining unit, inevitably, special circumstances will exist where treatment which is reasonable for the entire group is inappropriate for a specific case. The more diversity in the bargaining unit, and/or the more detailed the agreement, the more frequently this will occur. Teacher organizations that choose collective bargaining have chosen uniformity of treatment under previously agreed upon rules rather than individualization of treatment in special circumstances. That choice may be an improvement in some schools. But it may be regretted in others.

The Binding Nature of the Agreement

Once ratified by both parties, negotiated agreements, with only very special exceptions, are legally binding. The obligations incurred by the two parties, as well as the rights and benefits conferred, must be scrupulously observed. Carefully negotiated agreements will have been worded with extreme care to insure precision in communication of the nature of that agreement. Every word, every punctuation mark, in the agreement must be considered to exist for a specific purpose. Only damage to the continuing employment relationship can result from actions by either party based upon loose construction of the negotiated agreement. Both are required to act strictly in conformity with its exact language.

Temptation will arise when seemingly no harm to either party will result from "fudging" the agreement or ignoring an aspect of it that brings temporary discomfort to one or both parties. Such temptations must be resisted. If either party is not willing to conduct the affairs of the school in exact conformity with the specific language of the agreement, that language should be modified prior to ratification. Once signed, all parties are obliged to abide strictly by its terms.

Specific Time Limits

Earlier, an analogy was suggested comparing employment relations under a negotiated agreement to marriage. There is an important difference, however. The negotiated agreement is not "until death do us part." Normally it covers a period of from one to, perhaps, three years, and then lapses. When this occurs, a new understanding must be negotiated, and this takes place through the same process of collective bargaining that produced the expired agreement. Technically, nothing in the old agreement exists the moment its time span has elapsed. Nevertheless, the content of the previous agreement, and the experience of both parties under it, will have an important impact upon the negotiation of the successor agreement.

The content of the previous agreement will largely be carried over into the new agreement. That content has defined the basis for working together of the teachers and the representatives of their employer. Where both are satisfied with the existing relationship, both will wish to renegotiate the same terms and conditions. Where one or the other is dissatisfied with the existing agreement, change will be sought. Normally, teacher representatives will feel pressure from their membership to negotiate improvements in salary, benefits, and working conditions. Their approach to a successor agreement will be to hold onto what was desirable in the old and add to it improvements for the future. Administration representatives may find that the old agreement contained some elements that caused undue problems in administration. In such cases, they properly can and should propose revisions.

However, experience teaches administrators that revisions in existing agreements are generally resisted by teacher representatives. Where such modifications are made, they are made at the cost of concessions on additional salary or benefits. In negotiations, no agreement is apt to be achieved without some cost.

Whether the agreement will be in force for a single year or for a longer period must be negotiated between the parties. Often employees fear long-term agreements. Inflation can quickly erode salary gains. So prudence dictates having frequent opportunities for a new deal. Negotiations are costly, however, in time and effort. A longer-term agreement may be desirable from that standpoint. Sometimes a long-term agreement is negotiated with a "wage reopener." In such cases, everything but salaries is fixed for a two-or three-year term. That one issue is subject to renegotiation after one year.

One clear benefit to administration from a longer-term agreement is stability. This makes it possible to plan with greater confidence. A three-year agreement, for instance, makes long-range budget projections much more feasible than a succession of one-year agreements with the accompanying uncertainty about future operational costs. On the other hand, longer-range agreements can hurt administration since unanticipated changes in enrollment or curriculum needs often require changed operations. The negotiated agreement can severely limit the flexibility of administration to deploy faculty or modify programs. Since one cannot be sure what the future may bring, long-term rigid commitments are worrisome to administration.

The length of the agreement may have implications for the security of the union or association that represents the teachers. Either law or negotiated agreement may include a contract bar. This guarantees the union or association that its members cannot replace it with another bargaining agent for the life of the negotiated agreement. This consideration is especially valuable to an organization facing the possibility of a strong challenge from a contending organization. In such a case, the association may desire the long-term agreement for its own security. The employer may share this concern. Or the employer may want to provide teachers with an opportunity to change representatives.

PROBLEMS OF INTERPRETATION OF THE AGREEMENT

As has been discussed, teachers, administrators, and the board of education are bound to strict observance of the agreement during the agreed-upon period of time. But what constitutes that agreement? A written document exists. It is not the agreement, however. The agreement existed in the minds of the two negotiating teams at the time they shook hands and concluded their discussion on a point. The written document was prepared subsequent to that fleeting moment. Even in that brief time, some distortion may begin to creep into the minds of those involved as their recollections of the agreement begin to age. The writing of the agreement represents an effort on the part of each to find words and put them on paper to express the nature of that which was agreed to. Lewis Carroll had Humpty Dumpty say, "When *I* use a word, it means just what I choose it to mean—neither more nor less." So it is with negotiators!

Misunderstandings between Negotiators

It is quite possible that the negotiators, with all good intentions, simply misunderstood each other. While both may have thought they were in agreement, each attached some understanding to the words used that modified the agreement beyond what the other would have accepted had he thoroughly understood the meaning ascribed. Differences may exist, for instance, in the interpretation of *free period,* or *emergency,* or *promptly,* or of countless other words that may appear in the agreement. When such misunderstandings come about, a word or a phrase in the agreement possesses different meanings for the representative of the teachers and the representative of the employers. Often the very existence of this disagreement is not discovered until sometime later, when a teacher asks for something or takes some action. The administration cites the negotiated agreement as a basis for denial. The teacher inquires of the bargaining agent and is told that administration is wrong, that that was not what they agreed to at the bargaining table. Misunderstandings lead to disputes, and often to charges of dissimulation. From such incidents damaged employee relations grow.

Misunderstandings by Employees and Administrators

The agreement was negotiated and reduced to writing by representatives of the employees and of the employer. Most teachers and administrators were not directly involved in the process. Their understanding of the nature of the agreement is a result of the meaning they ascribe to the words in the document. And this meaning may not be quite what was intended by either set of negotiators. So the potential for disputes about the nature of the understanding between the parties is multiplied by the number of individuals who have occasion to interpret it. This problem is exacerbated by the fact that even the most perceptive set of negotiators can hardly be expected to anticipate every possible circumstance which might occur relative to some portion of their agreement. The unanticipated circumstance, when it does arise, requires teachers and administrators alike to guess what the negotiators would have agreed on as a fair resolution of such a case if they had anticipated its occurrence. Predictably, both parties will make such an estimate in a manner most favorable to their immediate concern. Equally predictable, the interpretations will differ. Continuing discussions throughout the life of the agreement can resolve many such misunderstandings.

Misunderstanding from Ambiguous Language

Differing shadings of meaning are likely to be given even the most careful chosen words. Sloppy construction of the language of the agreement will result in many other words by their very nature being subject to different interpretations. When the immediate welfare of a party is advanced by a favorable interpretation of ambiguous wording, one can predict favorable interpretation. Too much cannot be said for the value of careful construction and precision in word choice to insure clarity of expression of intent in the agreement.

A dilemma may exist, however. Precision may not lend itself to agreement, even though it is desirable in the administration of the agreement. Sometimes, especially when deadlines press the negotiators, they find that fuzzy language enables them to hide potential disagreement and so makes it possible for them to put together a document for ratification. Insistence upon clarity would highlight lingering disagreement. The choice becomes, Shall we have an agreement we both seek at the cost of sweeping some of our differences under the rug of ambiguity, or shall we risk failure to agree in order to achieve precision on a point that may never be a real issue in the operation of the schools?

GRIEVANCES: THE JUDICIAL MECHANISM

Since so many factors conspire to create misunderstanding and dispute among the parties to the agreement, a means is needed to resolve those disputes. The grievance process serves admirably. It is not too much to say that successful day-to-day administration of a negotiated agreement is impossible without the inclusion of an agreed-upon means to resolve differences of opinion about the specifics of that agreement.

Many teachers became familiar with a grievance process as they experience collective bargaining. The two are closely related. However, a grievance process is useful with or without collective negotiations. Carefully drawn grievance and/or formalized complaint procedures are a mark of good personnel administration under any circumstances.

Where administrators believe that individual employees should have a clearly understood means by which they can call the attention of superiors to circumstances which they believe to be unfair, a lubrication of the employment relationship exists. Where employees have no specified means for hearing and possible redress, smoldering discontents are likely.

Definition of a Grievance

No generally applicable definition of what constitutes a grievance is possible. Each negotiated agreement that provides a grievance procedure will define the nature of a grievance. One must look at a given agreement for the answer to the question, Is this a legitimate grievance?

Some grievances are defined solely in terms of the negotiated agreement itself. Since interpretation of the agreement is the primary function of a grievance procedure, this definition satisfies the major need. Only an allegation that the negotiated agreement has been interpreted unfairly or administered inequitably is a grievance.

In other cases, the definition is expanded to include an allegation that some board-of-education policy other than that of the negotiated agreement was applied inequitably or unfairly. A still broader definition would also include treatment that varied from past practice. This definition reflects the belief that employees are entitled to expect favorable tradition or precedent to be binding in making decisions about matters which concern them.

Some agreements define grievance so broadly as to include virtually any action of the employer or his representative that an employee believes to be unfair. This may even include the failure to take an action or have a policy the absence of which has resulted in inequity.

No prescription for good practice is warranted. Desirable relations and an understood means for resolving teachers' concerns are important goals of a well-operated school. The decision about the breadth of grievance definition must be considered within that framework.

Difference between a Grievance and a Complaint

Some districts have found that two parallel processes are desirable. In these cases, a grievance is defined narrowly. Then, another similar process is created and labeled a complaint procedure. The definition of a complaint is so broad in such cases that almost any dissatisfaction of a teacher has a procedural remedy. The reasons for the twin mechanisms will be clarified after discussion of the steps in processing grievances.

The discussion to this point may mislead the reader into believing that only an individual teacher can have a legitimate grievance. If so, that needs correction. Grievances may exist between an individual and his or her immediate supervisor, usually the principal. They may exist between groups of teachers and a principal. They may exist between the teacher organization as a corporate body and some member of the administration without affecting any individual teacher. Or they may exist between any of the above and the board of education, the legal employer, without involving any administrator. In practice, however, most grievances occur when an individual teacher believes that some decision or action of his immediate superior violates the terms of the negotiated agreement. The role of the teacher organization is more frequently that of advocate for the teacher than direct participant.

PROCESSING GRIEVANCES

The negotiated agreement, if it is well drawn, will provide for steps of appeal for individuals who believe themselves to have been treated inequitably. Details of processing at each step need to be established.

Informal Hearing

Grievances frequently occur because a difference in understanding the terms of the agreement exists between a principal and a teacher. Often this can be cleared up if the two meet and talk out the problem in an informal manner. It is quite common for the agreement to specify that the teacher may ask someone, often a representative of the teacher organization to accompany him to such an informal hearing. Administrators, too, usually ask another administrator to be present. The give-and-take of discussion may bring one to understand and accept the interpretation of the other. If so, the matter is resolved.

If the teacher still believes an injustice to be present, his next step is to file a formal written statement with the principal. Often this must include a precise statement of the portion of the negotiated agreement alleged to have been violated, a detailing of the nature of the violation, and the remedy sought. A desirable grievance clause will specify time limits bearing upon both parties. The teacher or the teacher organization will be limited so that an alleged grievance must be formally filed within a reasonable period of time after the grievant knew, or should have known, of the action resulting in the grievance. The principal and other representatives of the employer, throughout successive appeals, will be required to respond within a reasonable period of time.

Appeal to Higher Levels of Authority

In most cases, an appeal to the superintendent of schools or his designate constitutes the second level of grievance processing. The written statement of the grievant is forwarded, along with the written reply of the principal. The superintendent may hold a formal hearing at which both the principal and the aggrieved teacher, as well as the teacher-organization representative, are present. In a manner similar to that of the first level, the facts are sought and a written decision rendered. If the teacher and/or the teacher organization is satisfied with this response, the grievance has been settled. If not, the same process may be repeated on appeal to the board of education.

In many negotiated agreements, the decision of the board, as the employer, is final. In others, appeal for a binding decision by an outside impartial arbitrator is provided for. Serious issues are implicit in either case.

Those who believe that the board of education ought to make the final decision cite as their reason the board's role in the determination of public policy. The negotiated agreement is, upon ratification, official board-of-education policy. Only the board of education, composed of the elected representatives of the public, is authorized to act for the state legislature in establishing policy for public education. This argument hinges on the judgment that any decision contrary to that of the board as to the meaning of the negotiated agreement would itself be an establishment of policy. Opponents of binding arbitration believe that only the duly authorized representatives of the public, accountable to the public through normal democratic processes, can and should be empowered to make public policy.

Others disagree. Employment relations, they argue, is a special case. When legislatures require or permit boards of education to engage in collective bargaining, the legislatures implicitly accept the bilateral nature of that relationship. The board and the organization representing the teachers are equals in the matter of determining employment relationships. Thus, a disagreement between these equals cannot be settled unilaterally by one of them and still maintain that balance of power. Advocates of impartial binding arbitration believe that the entire process of collective bargaining rests on the consent of employees and employer to continue their relationship on terms each has accepted as reasonable. If one party decides what the agreement is to mean and forces that decision upon the other, they hold, the element of consent is irrevocably destroyed.

Those with this belief argue that where misunderstandings or differences of opinion about the meaning of the agreement occur after the agreement was consummated, fairness requires impartial arbitrator determination.

A Single- or a Two-Track System?

Widespread agreement exists that where outside binding arbitration exists, the role of the arbitrator must be limited to deciding what the agreement means. Arbitration does not permit an outsider to substitute his judgment for that of the parties who negotiated the agreement. The arbitrator may not decide what the agreement should have been. He may be barred from an opinion of what would be a desirable resolution of the difficulty. He is limited to an interpretation of the intent of the negotiators as this is revealed in the agreement itself.

This understanding makes it possible for binding arbitration to be used to decide what the wording of a contract means. However, teacher dissatisfaction that is not a matter of disagreement about the interpretation of a clause in the negotiated agreement can hardly be resolved by outside interpretation. School systems that have established a double-track system have agreements in which grievances are subject to outside binding arbitration. Complaints—that is, employee allegations of injustice which cannot be resolved by interpretation of the agreement —have their final appeal to the board of education.

RESPONSIBILITIES OF THE TWO PARTIES

The agreement establishes a set of responsibilities governing relations between the two parties. If the agreement is to work well in practice, each party must also fulfill a related set of obligations to its own constituency.

The constituency of the negotiators for the board is the board itself and its administrative agency. Principals, assistant principals, directors, and other supervisors throughout the school system must think and act on behalf of the board as representatives in the field in the day-to-day administration of the negotiated agreement.

Where exclusive recognition is in force, the constituency of the bargaining agent comprises all the members of the bargaining unit it represents. Sometimes misunderstandings arise in this regard. It should be clear, however, that the assumption of the position of exclusive representative means the assumption of the obligation to represent all within the bargaining unit regardless of whether or not they are members of the union or association that serves as bargaining agent. Failure to provide the same level of representation for members and nonmembers alike is subject to action as an unfair labor practice, and could result in decertification.

Agreements are negotiated in an adversary relationship. The administration of the agreement should proceed in the same manner. As in negotiations, an adversary relationship need not imply hostility. But there are two sides to the bargain, and two sets of priorities and concerns to be guarded. Both administration and the bargaining agent have responsibilities to those they represent. These responsibilities will sustain the adversary posture, but can and should be discharged with businesslike dispassion. Trust that one's opposite number will behave with integrity is not at all the same thing as a blind assumption that one's opposite number will look out for one's own responsibilities. A well-administered agreement is more likely to result from a constructive tension in which both pay close attention to their own concerns.

Responsibilities of the Teacher Organization

Teachers, members of the bargaining unit, have every right to expect diligent attention from their representatives. The following list summarizes at least the most pressing of these responsibilities.

1. To provide means by which teachers can become familiar with their rights under the agreement.
2. To provide machinery for appropriate interaction with the administration where the agreement establishes consultation rights. One common form of this is through building committees, which share, in agreed-upon ways, in the decision-making process.
3. To monitor the agreement to ensure full implementation of all aspects of it favorable to the interests of teachers.

4. To provide for continuous evaluation of the agreement in operation as a basis for planning proposals to be advanced at the next round of negotiations.
5. To secure the most favorable possible interpretation of ambiguous aspects of the agreement.
6. To provide counsel and support to all members of the bargaining unit who have a grievance.
7. To provide whatever funds may be required under the agreement to cover costs of arbitration of grievances.

Responsibilities of Administration

In a similar fashion, those in administration who bear primary responsibility for employment relations have obligations to the employing board of education and to other administrators.

1. To ensure understanding of the details of the agreement by all those who will act in a supervisory capacity in its administration.
2. To ensure that the agreement is monitored so that all obligations of teachers are fulfilled.
3. To provide for continuous evaluation of the impact of the agreement upon learning and upon the efficient operation of the schools as a basis for developing needed proposals for change during the next round of negotiations.
4. To ensure understanding by administrators of the means by which grievance claims are to be processed.
5. To ensure knowledge by all administrators of precedents in the interpretation of the agreement as these are established by decisions of other administrators, especially in response to grievances.
6. To provide advice and support to administrators against whom grievances have been filed.
7. To demonstrate conclusively that the filing of grievances against decisions of administrators will not be used as a basis for evaluation of the performance of those administrators.

SUMMARY

Unlike an economic transaction, the conclusion of negotiations is the beginning of a continuing relationship. Both parties to the agreement will coexist under the agreed-upon terms for a specified period of time. The satisfaction of teachers, and the success of the school in fulfilling its responsibilities to pupils and to society, rests in part upon the effectiveness with which the negotiated agreement can be translated into day-to-day employment relations at the school-building level.

Not every contingency can be provided for in negotiating an agreement. Not every possibility for misunderstanding can be avoided in the wording of the agreement. A carefully planned grievance procedure is a vital element in the agreement. Its intelligent use by both parties will contribute to the maintenance of good employment relations.

An agreement establishes obligations for both its signatories. Some of these are to each other, some are implied to the constituents of each. Good bargains rest, finally, on the integrity of both parties in their implementation.

CHAPTER 6

The Written Agreement

The physical product of collective negotiations is a document. In it, the representatives of the teachers and the employing board of education spell out in some detail the basis for their continued employment relations. The purpose of this chapter is to consider the nature of such documents and to study the component parts which are usually present.

NATURE OF THE AGREEMENT

Examination of agreements between teacher organizations and employing boards of education reveals that there are wide variations among them. Some are brief and general. Some are complex and lengthy. Agreements have been negotiated where the board of education apparently was in full concurrence with the teachers in believing that the process of negotiations was good for the schools. Others have been negotiated with boards of education that were present at the bargaining table only under the compulsion of law.

Enforcement of the Agreement

One question which arises early is, Will the agreement be enforceable in court? An answer to this must be hedged until one is familiar with the legislation in the particular state concerned. Where legislation requires boards of education to negotiate, defines unfair labor practices, and creates administrative machinery to umpire the process, the answer is probably yes. Appeals from decisions of administrative agencies normally can be made to the courts, so the arbitrator of employment disputes in such cases is the legal system.

However, the case is not so clear where no legislative mandate forces the employing board into the collective-bargaining relationship. In such a case, the board has decided to negotiate as a means by which personnel policy is to be considered. This decision was a voluntary one made unilaterally by the board. Should the board in such a case decide to choose another means of determining employment-relations policies, it could, of course, do so. In such a case, it is quite possible that the courts would rule that the act of engaging in collective negotiations represents the present policy of the board and is subject to change at the discretion of the board. Hence a board could set aside negotiations procedures, and perhaps the agreements resulting from them, at whatever time it felt the welfare of the schools required it.

In the absence of legislation, a negotiated agreement may be more like a treaty between two nations than a contract between two parties. As is the case with treaties, both sides must consider the possible consequences of abrogation. Hence, boards may continue an agreement in force even though they might like to drop it because they fear the consequences of default more than the inconveniences of compliance.

Regardless of the presence or absence of legislation, however, teacher organizations often refer to the product of negotiations as a contract. In most usages, the term *contract* implies that one party will provide some goods or services to another for a stipulated price. This is certainly not the case in an employment-relations agreement. Teacher organizations negotiate on behalf of the members of the bargaining unit. They do not agree to furnish teachers directly to provide professional services. The section of teachers and their direction and supervision, as has been previously discussed, are functions retained by the employing board and exercised through its administration. A teacher organization is not an educational contractor. It is the representative of the members of a bargaining unit.

Extent of Agreement

A negotiated agreement can hardly anticipate every possible issue that may arise during its term. Where the level of suspicion is high between teachers and employing boards and/or administration, attempts to do this are made however. These attempts result in very long, detailed agreements, which try to build in a rule for every conceivable circumstance.

Other agreements are less detailed and rest predominantly on an understanding of the mutual interest of teachers and school boards in effective schools. Where both parties believe that shared involvement in decisions provides long-run benefits, an atmosphere of collegiality can develop. In such cases, the collectively negotiated agreement is more like a constitution than a contract. It serves to communicate in broad terms the shared nature of the collective effort in providing educational services to a community. Such an agreement establishes a framework for continued interaction on a regularized basis between the representative of the teachers and the administration of the schools. It assumes that the problems which arise can and will be resolved as each party accepts a continuing good-faith responsibility to work together in order to maintain the mutual enterprise.

MINIMUM REQUIREMENTS OF AN AGREEMENT

What must be present to constitute a negotiated agreement is open to dispute. At varying times all kinds of documents have been called agreements; some have been as little as a paragraph in the minutes of the local board of education signifying that the board intended to meet with the representatives of the teachers. As teacher organizations and boards have grown in experience with the negotiations process, however, restrictive definitions have been accepted. The following inclusions seem necessary to achieve what many would accept as a negotiated agreement.

Recognition

A clause which officially recognizes a specific organization as the representative of a specifically defined bargaining unit is necessary. This serves to define the parties to the agreement and the makeup of the bargaining unit. Where the teacher organization is the exclusive representative, such relationship is agreed to in this clause. Often, a statement binding the parties to take no action inconsistent with the agreement is included.

Negotiation Procedures

Several matters are frequently included in this section. The duration of the agreement is fixed. Since the agreement is for a specified time, but exists in anticipation of a longer continuing relationship, provisions for the negotiation of a successor agreement need to be specified. Provision should be made for notification of the other party in ample time to permit adequate preparations for new negotiations. A statement which formalizes the understanding that matters contained in the agreement are not subject to further negotiation for the life of that agreement may be desired. This is sometimes called a zipper clause.

Salary and Benefits

Since collective negotiations exist in order to provide bilateral policy formation of wages, hours, and terms and conditions of employment, an agreement could hardly exist without stipulation of at least salary and benefit plans. These two, taken together, may be termed compensation. The particular mix in which teachers receive compensation directly through salary or take relatively less compensation in salary and more of it in employer-paid benefits must be decided by the membership of teacher organizations and then negotiated at the table. Income tax considerations enter into this question. Comparisons of agreements in other school districts cannot be made simply by comparing salaries. Total compensation, salary plus employer-paid benefits, is a more accurate basis. Unfortunately, this comparison is not easily made.

Grievance Procedures

Grievance procedures provide the judicial mechanism necessary in order to give operational definition to the language of the agreement. An agreement without this provision could hardly be put into effect since the agreement would evaporate at the first dispute as to its meaning. Grievance avoids this, and consequently is necessary to give continuing viability to the agreement. Legislation in Pennsylvania permits the parties to negotiations to work out what they believe to be a wise grievance procedure. But the law also requires that whatever form this may take, it must conclude with binding arbitration. In this fashion, the law requires a definitive means to resolve disputes over the meaning of the agreement.

The requirement that grievances be answered within a specified period of time is equally necessary. Without this protection, an uncooperative administration could subvert the intent of grievance by simply ignoring claims.

COMPREHENSIVE AGREEMENTS

Experience in bargaining demonstrates that as time passes, agreements become more extensive. Additional articles representing additional employee concerns are pressed for once the minimum aspects of a negotiated agreement have been achieved.

Hours

Since "wages, hours, and terms and conditions of employment" are basic to collective negotiations, one would think that little problem would exist in determining negotiability here. But public education has a special circumstance. Schools, generally speaking, are not in year-round session.

The negotiability of daily time requirements is well established. Problems do occur in deciding what is the legitimate extent of teacher responsibility for participation in meetings and staff-development activities beyond the pupil day. But the give-and-take of negotiations provides a means by which such disputes can be settled.

A more difficult problem exists in determining whether the requirement to negotiate "hours" implies a requirement of the board to negotiate the length of the school year and the extent of vacation periods. Is the calendar a determination of the amount of time an employee is required to perform services? If that is the case, then the question is a matter of "hours" and must be agreed to by the teachers' representatives. On the other hand, is the length of the school year and the amount of vacation time a matter of deciding the extent of program and services the school district will provide students? If that is the case, then it appears that this is a matter of policy determination reserved to the sole authority of the board. As such it is not subject to required negotiations. The school calendar determines both. This situation has no real parallel in the history of industrial relations. Industrial bargaining precedents are not helpful, and new precedents for education remain yet to be established.

Other Terms and Conditions of Employment

What "other terms and conditions of employment" means in public-education circumstances is even in more dispute than the previous issue of hours. This phrase is also borrowed from industrial experience. However, in industry, generally speaking, the phrase refers to the physical conditions under which labor works. The achievement of clean, safe, healthful working conditions is, and has been, a matter of real concern in many industries. The right to negotiate in attempts to secure such conditions is recognized.

Teachers in public schools generally do not have this concern. While some situations hardly bring complacency about the possibility of physical harm to teachers, most teachers work under physical circumstances that cause few real problems. Teachers have generally interpreted this phrase much more broadly than industrial workers. Teachers are concerned about professional matters relating to the means by which education is provided in a community. The typical assembly-line worker is not apt to feel a sense of personal responsibility for the quality or design of the product of his labors. Teachers care very much about the quality of education.

Professional educators have professional concerns. These concerns encompass such issues as the nature of the curriculum, the materials of instruction, the adequacy of the library, the nature of disciplinary policies, the size of classes, and the professional-development activities of the district. Few board members, administrators, teachers, or parents would want teachers to be unconcerned with these issues. What kind of faculty would it be which washed its hands of concern for the way education was provided in a community?

The issue is not whether these are legitimate concerns. The issue is whether these are inherent working conditions and so the proper subject for bargaining. Teacher organizations have answered these questions with an emphatic yes. What could be more a matter of working conditions than the circumstances under which teachers and students come together? Boards have frequently said no! They argue that the kind and quality of educational services in a public school must be determined by the public through its representatives. Most agree that teachers should have an opportunity to offer professional opinions on such matters. But many draw the line at agreeing that the bargaining table is the proper site for deciding them. The difference lies in the fact that if such issues are subject to negotiation, teacher organizations will have a voice equal to that of the board in their resolution.

As in the case of the school calendar, it is too early in the development of collective negotiations in public education for a clear picture to have emerged. Much more argumentation and litigation will ensue before anyone will be able to define what "other conditions of employment" means in public education.

Representation of Individual Teachers

In the process of negotiating an agreement, the teacher organization represents teachers collectively. Some agreements include a clause which authorizes teachers to have a representative from the union or association present at any conference with a principal or other administrator that may result in some action unfavorable to the teacher. This has a double benefit to teachers. They are assured of support if a reprimand or negative evaluation is possibly forthcoming. This support provides the advantage of an uninvolved person who can perhaps offer explanation or argument in behalf or the teacher more effectively than the emotionally involved teacher himself. Secondly, it provides a basis for a procedural defense. A form of due process is guaranteed. If the principal does not adhere strictly to these requirements, the facts of the case may not be usable in later disciplinary action.

Provisions for Leave of Absence

Several kinds of leave are provided for in various agreements. The most common is sick leave, if state statutes do not take precedence. Maternity leaves are frequently found. Recent court decisions have sharply restricted the limitations and requirements previously established by boards of education relative to maternity leaves. Leave for military service and jury duty are sometimes included. Death in the family and similar emergency-leave provisions are found in many agreements.

Study leaves or sabbatical-leave provisions have been included in some cases. These provisions require considerable care in negotiation to insure that a number of important questions are adequately considered. Criteria for determination of eligibility must be spelled out. Compensation during the leave must be established. Requirements that teachers return to service in the district granting the leave are not uncommon. Specific understandings about employer contributions to retirement and insurance programs during the time of the leave are important.

Access to Personnel Files

Fear of damaging error or possible malice resulting in professionally harmful inclusions in personnel records have led to clauses in negotiated agreements which ensure that the teacher may, upon reasonable notice, review his own personnel file. Some agreements prevent the inclusion of any material not directly bearing upon the teaching performance of the individual. Frequently, to prohibit anonymous material, provision is made that material included in the file must be signed by the individual making the report, who thus attests to its accuracy.

Provisions for teachers to review files are strengthened when the teacher has the right to file a response to any material included in his file. In large systems more than one teacher may have the same name. Errors of misfiling can be guarded against by teacher access and review rights.

Teacher organizations are fearful of secret personnel files in which material is kept about which the teacher is unaware. Provisions that prevent the administration from using any material not included in the regular personnel file give protection in this regard.

Some difficulty in administering these provisions exists in the case of letters of recommendation and placement papers. Universities which prepare and distribute sets of recommendations about applicants for placement purposes, often require that the material be kept confidential from the teacher. These requirements protect the confidentiality of appraisals of fitness and promise. Universities reason that the teacher will be helped to find employment when the potential employer knows that the information about the candidate has been given with candor. Placement papers are often retained by the employing district after the applicant is employed. If they are kept in the personnel file, and if access to the personnel file is guaranteed by the negotiated agreement, the district violates the confidentiality which the university has promised those who prepared letters of recommendation. Procedures can be developed which solve this problem, but a number of districts have yet to give sufficient attention to the issue.

ORGANIZATIONAL SECURITY

Basic agreements as well as comprehensive ones often include a category of stipulations which are different in kind from those previously mentioned. These agreements benefit the organization representing teachers rather than teachers themselves. A concern of an employee organization is its own welfare. Clauses of this type are called organizational-security clauses.

Membership Requirements

The life-blood of an organization is its membership growth and retention. With membership comes dues, the necessary funds to support organizational activities. Further, membership brings a measure of bargaining power. The employer is less apt to be responsive to an organization which appears to lack support from those it purports to represent.

Membership requirements are agreements specifying that the employer will discharge any employee who violates them. Several membership requirements, which exist, or existed in the past, in industrial unionism, are widely accepted as inappropriate in public education.

The closed shop, which requires union membership as a condition of initial employment, is no longer legal in private industry. The union shop, which requires employees to join the union within a period of time after employment or be fired, has not been accepted in public education.

The agency shop is a variation of this, however, which has been included in agreements between boards and the representatives of teachers. Agency-shop agreements require that teachers either join the organization that represents them in bargaining or, if they prefer not to join, pay a fee to cover a share of the costs of operating the organization.

Teacher organizations and their members resent what they term freeloaders. Teachers who are part of the bargaining unit must receive all benefits negotiated for that unit regardless of their membership in the organization. Organizations are required to provide the same representation services in cases of grievances irrespective of the membership status of teachers. These services cost. Unions, understandably, feel it desirable to have a guarantee that those who benefit from their services will pay a share of the costs.

Others disagree as a matter of principle. They hold that retention or dismissal of teachers ought to be based upon no factor other than the possession of proper certification and demonstrated performance. They point out the long history of the struggle for tenure, which guarantees dismissal only for a stated cause bearing upon teaching competence. Dismissal for refusal to pay fees to a bargaining agent, they say, is an intolerable infringement upon the principles of tenure, violates existing tenure laws, and destroys the professional status of teachers.

Maintenance-of-membership agreements require teachers who are members of a bargaining agent at the time an agreement is negotiated to remain members for the life of that agreement. Teacher organizations see this as a protection against the possibility that teachers, once the benefits of a negotiated agreement are secured, may refuse to pay further dues and drop their membership. With assured income the union can make commitments and develop programs. One other consequence of maintenance-of-membership clauses is that a situation is created where the self-interest of the teacher organization is related to longer agreements.

Other Security Provisions

Dues check-off arrangements are agreements whereby the employing board undertakes to withhold dues from the paychecks of organization members and transmit those funds directly to the teacher organization. Individual teachers must request that this be done. The union is saved the cost and inconvenience of dues collection by such an agreement. Further, it ensures the regularity of the organization's income.

Officers of teacher organizations must devote considerable amounts of time to conducting the business of the organization. Some agreements provide for leaves of absence for officers so that their full time can be devoted to organization business. Other clauses may make provision for substitutes and the guarantee of no salary reduction for time absent from classes on specified organizational business.

Teacher organizations have received rights to bulletin-board space in schools, to use mail boxes and interschool delivery facilities, and sometimes to insert notices in daily school bulletins. These provisions obviously make it cheaper and easier for the organization to conduct its business.

The negotiated agreement exists between the teacher organization as a corporate entity and the employing board of education. Some portions of agreements exist to protect the interests of the organization in maintaining the provisions of the agreement above and beyond the concerns of individual teachers. Where a grievance is processed between the teacher and the employer, the teacher is not normally required to be represented by the bargaining agent if he does not wish representation. Of course, the teacher may not substitute the services of a minority teacher organization where the majority representative has exclusive representation status. But the teacher could process the grievance without representation. Anticipating such cases, teacher organizations often write into the agreement a clause which protects their right to be present at the discussions. The purpose of this is to assure that the accommodation worked out by the employer and the individual teacher does not establish a precedent detrimental to the interests of the representative organization.

SUMMARY

The written agreement between an employing board of education and the representative of teachers in a bargaining unit is the product of the collective negotiations. This agreement may be simple, focused upon establishing general understandings as to the ways the two parties will work together in their continuing relationship. Or it may be complex, binding each to carefully drawn stipulations which attempt to guard prerogatives and secure protections each believe necessary to their safety.

The parties to the agreement, the duration of the agreement, the makeup of the bargaining unit covered, and the means of negotiating a successor agreement are necessary parts of any agreement. Compensation plans are a basic inclusion. Grievance procedures are necessary in order that the agreement can function. These elements make up any complete negotiated agreement.

More complex agreements include understandings of the time required of teachers, representation rights, leave-of-absence provisions, and rights of access to personnel files. Considerable dispute exists about the extension of bargaining to other issues of importance to teachers. Teacher organizations insist that all aspects of professional concern for education are properly included as "other terms and conditions of employment." Boards of education often resist extension of the meaning of this phrase beyond the physical conditions under which teaching is performed.

Three separate interests are represented in the act of bargaining: the interests of teachers, the interests of employing boards, the interests of the teacher organization as an institution. Organizational-security clauses in agreements protect the legitimate concern of the teacher organization for its own survival and growth in order that it have the necessary strength to maintain the balance of power necessary for effective collective negotiations.

CHAPTER 7

A Lot May Change

Fair consideration of the process of collective negotiations in public education requires one to keep in mind that our experience in this area is brief and rapidly evolving. Most school districts are still well within their first decade of experience with this method of determining board-of-education policy. Large sections of our country have had virtually no experience with it. This rapid evolution teaches that the present is a shaky basis for definitive commentary. Events yet to transpire will undoubtedly affect collective negotiations in ways that can now only be speculated upon.

Six developing circumstances have potential for significant modification of the practice of collective negotiations for teachers. Detailed consideration of these circumstances is beyond the scope of this book. But mention seems necessary to provide a context for thinking about what the future may hold for employment relationships.

STATEWIDE FINANCING OF PUBLIC EDUCATION

Court cases in California, Texas, and New Jersey have focused public attention on the question of equality of opportunity in public education. A central issue which has surfaced may be stated this way. Does equal protection of the law require that equal financial resources support the public-education opportunity of every child within a state? This issue is both a legal and a political one. It may be decided by courts, or by legislatures, or by both. The solution may take the form of state-wide financing so that equal amounts of money are available for every child regardless of where in the state he or she may live.

If funds for public education are to be equalized by statewide financing, what will that imply for collective bargaining? Two possible responses appear logical.

The first is to shift the locus of bargaining from the individual district to the state. Statewide bargaining suggests statewide master agreements. While some aspects of work relationships might still remain to be negotiated at the local level, much of the hard give-and-take of bargaining would be undertaken by representatives of the legislature and statewide teacher organizations. Whether this would take the form of bilateral, across-the-table bargaining, as has been described in this book, or be more like traditional lobbying activity can only be speculated about.

The second possibility is that bargaining would continue to take place at the local level. In this case, the amount of money allocated to the various needs of the district would be predetermined. Bargaining would deal with the extent to which portions of these funds would be allocated to salaries, benefits, and other needs. This would, of course, suggest that every dollar gained for teacher welfare would be at the expense of other legitimate needs, such as libraries, laboratory supplies, textbooks, and so forth. Clearly this would be an uncomfortable position for teacher representatives.

MERGER

Talks have been underway for some years now exploring the possibility of merger between the two major teacher organizations, the National Education Association and the American Federation of Teachers. Merger has been consummated in New York. Nationwide formal merger into one giant union has proved difficult to achieve, but efforts continue.

Apart from freeing both organizations from the costs of competition for representation rights, merger suggests formidable political power. Both organizations now have formally organized political-action groups. Both agree on the desirability of action designed to elect officials friendly to public-education causes. Merger would create a very large union. Advocates of this course appear to feel that the long-term welfare of teachers would be better secured by the development and exercise of political power than from the attempt to negotiate improvements with local boards of education.

STAFF DIFFERENTIATION

More technical implications for collective negotiations may be coming as school districts move toward differentiation in the assignment of professional staff. Traditionally, teachers have been assigned responsibilities ranging from clerical work to diagnosis of learning disability. Specialization of assignment has been in terms of age of pupils taught and subject discipline. Little experience exists with specialization of function.

Interest has been indicated in making such distinctions, however. Staffing plans that provide levels of professional responsibility from intern teacher to master teacher have been proposed. Where these plans are adopted, certified teachers have quite different kinds of tasks and levels of responsibility. Further, teacher-aide personnel of various kinds are being widely utilized.

These staffing plans have implications for the development of bargaining units. As discussed previously, successful definition of a bargaining unit requires that the members of the unit have essentially the same employment relationships and potential employment concerns. Whether that would be the case between a master teacher, whose responsibilities would predominantly be in supervision and curriculum development, and an intern teacher, whose responsibilities would largely be in pupil assistance and control, is open to question. If the answer is no, then two or more bargaining units, each with its own organization, each negotiating separate agreements, would appear to be necessary. This fragmentation would suggest problems both for administration and for the separated teachers.

NEGOTIATIONS RIGHTS FOR ADMINISTRATORS

A related issue is the question of bargaining for administrators. The discussion in this book has been based upon the assumption that administration serves as an agency of the board of education in employment relations. The functions of supervision, administration of personnel, and enforcement of the negotiated agreement are carried out by administration as an agent for the board of education.

But what of the determination of wages, hours, and terms and conditions of employment for administrators? What about administrator participation in decision-making? How are these now to be determined? Some districts have avoided these issues. They have found it possible to assure the administrative staff that it did not need collective representation. A management-team approach has brought administrators into an intimate relationship with the board of education to the point that administrators feel themselves to be partners in the decision-making process. Boards of education have ensured that administrators are fully satisfied in their own economic concerns so that no need for a bargaining relationship is felt.

However desirable this relationship may be, it is, unfortunately, rare. Large city systems particularly have found it difficult to demonstrate to middle-level administration that its members are not simply employees of a large bureaucracy. Smaller systems have more potential for the creation of a management team, but full commitment to the concept is present in few boards of education. Consequently, middle-level administration, believing itself squeezed between aggressive bargainers for teachers and an uncaring or unaware board of education, has pressed for bargaining rights to protect its interests.

Legislation provides for some forms of formal representation in some states, and is under consideration in others. However, little experience exists to date. A board of education simultaneously bargaining with a strong, aggressive teacher organization and a separate, equally determined administrator organization, will undoubtedly have difficulty accommodating demands. On some issues, a natural difference of concern will exist. Then the board will be in a position of attempting to mediate between the conflicting demands of the two organizations. The conflict, in part, will be between the two organizations. The demands may be for guarantees by the board that certain concessions will not be made to the other organization.

FEDERAL LEGISLATION

Bills have been introduced in Congress that are designed to do for public employment what the Wagner Act did in the private sector. A federal law that would require collective negotiations and establish the ground rules under which negotiations would take place is sought. Proponents of this legislation point to the experience of negotiations in states that have adopted mandatory legislation. They argue that many states have not as yet enacted such legislation but will do so in the future. Federal legislation would make this unnecessary, and, further, would have the definite advantage of providing one set of rules over this important question rather than separate, sometimes partially conflicting legislation in each of the several states. Presumably, advocates of bargaining rights for teachers and other public employees also favor federal legislation because of disappointment with the pace of adoption of state legislation, for in many states such laws have not as yet, been passed.

Federal legislation would supplant existing state legislation. This is a matter of concern to some, especially in the matter of the legalized right to strike. Only three states, at the present time, authorize teacher strikes under any circumstances. Many provide harsh punishments for infraction of anti-strike legislation. Some who favor collective-bargaining rights for teachers still oppose federal legislation, fearing that if passed it would forbid strikes, and abort the possibility that favorable experience with legalization of the strike might cause legislation to spread to other states.

PUBLIC REPRESENTATION AT THE BARGAINING TABLE

Previous discussion in this book has identified the board of education as the representative of the public interest in the conduct of collective bargaining. However, the public, particularly parents, may not agree that its interests are adequately represented by the board. Parents recognize that the concerns of the board of education transcend the immediate question of impact on instruction. Issues in negotiation will predictably be considered in terms of their effect on the long-term maintenance of the school system; on the level of taxation in the community; on hopes for growth, or fear of reduction, of the industrial tax base of the community; and on the political concerns of members of the board of education. Parents of youngsters in school may well understand the concern of the board for these things but not share its priority of concern. In many issues, parental concerns may parallel those of the teacher organization more closely than those of the board. Thus, parents are often not willing to concede that their interests are adequately represented by the board of education. This is especially true in metropolitan cities, where few citizens know board members personally, and where the board may be composed of persons of different ethnic, economic, and social backgrounds than most of the parents.

As parents demand more direct participation, the bilateral nature of collective negotiations may be transformed into a trilateral model. This suggests bargaining behavior geared to the creation of alliances so that two parties can impose their will on the minority, rather than bargaining behavior of two equal adversaries. The form such interaction might take if implemented is as yet unknown.

As time passes, developments in these and other areas may well result in changed views about the nature of collective bargaining in public education. Indeed, formalized bargaining on a bilateral basis may prove unwieldy in public education. Future teacher organizations and boards of education may develop new, as yet unimagined ways by which matters of shared concern can be resolved. The strength of collective bargaining lies in the voluntary nature of the agreements it can produce. One may hope that increased experience in working together may lead teacher groups and boards of education to develop new processes for joint action by and for those whose interest is public education.

Bibliography

ACKERLY, ROBERT L., and JOHNSON, W. STANFIELD. *Critical Issues in Negotiations Legislation.* Professional Negotiations Pamphlets, No. 3. Washington: National Association of Secondary School Principals, 1969. This pamphlet examines the extremely important questions that arise when legislation is being considered.

American Association of School Administrators. *The School Administrator and Negotiation.* Washington: The Association, 1968. The association attempted in this book to set a tone and suggest general approaches to what was then a new problem. This is a helpful guide for administrators just beginning negotiations and a good recheck for those with experience.

CARLETON, PATRICK W., and GOODWIN, HAROLD I. *The Collective Dilemma: Negotiations in Education.* Worthington, Ohio: Jones Publishing Co., 1969. Three major parts and several subsections serve to organize the contributions of a variety of authors into a comprehensive book. This is an excellent overview of the topic.

DOHERTY, ROBERT E., and OBERER, WALTER E. *Teachers, School Boards and Collective Bargaining: A Changing of the Guard.* Ithaca: New York State School of Industrial and Labor Relations, 1967. Two established scholars in industrial relations with experience in public education blend these backgrounds in an engaging look at the developing phenomenon of bargaining in public education. Useful ideas about desirable legislation are included.

ELAM, STANLEY; LIEBERMAN, MYRON; and MOSKOW, MICHAEL H. *Readings on Collective Negotiations in Public Education.* Chicago: Rand McNally, 1967. A thorough compilation of the thinking of a number of authorities, written at the time negotiations activity was rapidly developing in the major metropolitan areas.

EPSTEIN, BENJAMIN. *The Principal's Role in Collective Negotiations.* Professional Negotiations Pamphlets, No. 1. Washington: National Association of Secondary School Principals, 1969. Mr. Epstein has been closely identified with principals and negotiations. This is a brief overview of a complex set of problems. The statement represents the position of NASSP.

GILROY, THOMAS P., et al. *Educator's Guide To Collective Negotiations.* Columbus: Charles E. Merrill, 1969. The authors speak to both parties to negotiations in public education. A case study is included to illustrate the process. Specific questions are posed and answered directly.

HAGBURG, EUGENE C. *Problems Confronting Union Organizations in Public Employment.* Columbus: Labor and Research Service, Ohio State University, 1966. This book is a collection of papers exploring various aspects of union problems. In "Teacher Collective Bargaining Today," David Selden, who until recently was president of AFT, provides a valuable view of his insights in this key office.

HENNESSY, MARY L., and WARNER, KENNETH O. *Public Management at the Bargaining Table.* Chicago: Public Personnel Association, 1967. This book has three main sections, treating the dynamics of collective bargaining, the bargaining process, and the future of collective bargaining. The purpose is to aid those with management responsibilities in public agencies.

JENSEN, VERNON H. "The Process of Collective Bargaining and the Question of its Obsolescence." *Industrial and Labor Review* 16 (July 1963): 546–56. This article succinctly but thoroughly establishes and defends the process of collective bargaining as consistent with our democratic heritage. The author warns against well-meaning persons who would interject a third force into bargaining and urges voluntary agreements developed by the parties.

KRAMER, LOUIS I. *Principals and Grievance Procedures.* Professional Negotiations Pamphlets No. 2. Worthington, Ohio: National Association of Secondary School Principals, 1969. Tips to principals, examples of grievance-clause wording, and alternative practices are included in this helpful brief discussion of the principal's responsibilities in handling grievances.

LAUTERBACH, HERBERT P., ed. *This Is How We Did It.* Harrisburg: Pennsylvania State Education Association, 1965. Over one hundred local associations report briefly on their efforts to provide effective programs for their memberships. At the time of publication few were engaged in formal collective bargaining, but efforts at membership enrollment, public relations, policy analysis, and teacher-benefit consideration are reported.

LIEBERMAN, MYRON, and MOSKOW, MICHAEL. *Collective Negotiations for Teachers.* Chicago: Rand McNally, 1966. Perhaps the most widely known book in the field. This is a massive volume which discusses the many problems and issues in detail. An excellent source for documents and materials relative to the development of bargaining in public education.

MARX, HERBERT L., ed. *Collective Bargaining for Public Employees.* New York: H. W. Wilson Co., 1969. A collection of reprinted articles that originally appeared in various professional journals. One article offers an alternative to collective negotiations in education.

MILLER, WILLIAM C., and NEWBURY, DAVID H. *Teacher Negotiation: A Guide for the Bargaining Team.* West Nyack, N.Y.: Parker Publishing Co., 1970. Two professional negotiators for boards of education in New York have written this book, which shares their opinions, their tactics, and their point of view toward negotiations.

National Commission on Teacher Education and Professional Standards. *Negotiating for Professionalization.* Washington: National Education Association, 1969. A booklet containing selected papers delivered to the 1969 National TEPS conference. Concern is shown for the problems in using the collective negotiation process effectively in educational institutions. No consistent theme is present, but useful points of view are offered.

National Education Association. *Guidelines for Professional Negotiation.* Washington: The Association, 1968. A brief handbook designed to recommend actions and guide decisions of local associations.

NIERENBERG, GERALD. *The Art of Negotiating.* New York: Hawthorne, 1968. The author has had an interesting career of negotiating business deals. Principles of effective negotiation are abstracted from this experience. While collective negotiation of employment conditions is a special case, much can be applied from the suggestions in this book.

NIGRO, FELIX, symposium ed. *Collective Negotiations in the Public Service. Public Administration Review* (1968). This issue of the American Society for Public Administration's journal is entirely devoted to a symposium on the impact of collective negotiations on the practice of personnel administration in public agencies. The five papers it contains treat the conceptual framework of negotiations practice with valuable insight.

PARKER, HYMAN; REPAS, BOB; and SCHMIDT, CHARLES. *A Guide to Collective Negotiations in Education.* East Lansing, Mich.: Social Science Research Bureau, 1967. Michigan was an early locus for collective bargaining in education. This short book was designed to assist boards of education in that state to prepare for their new responsibilities. The book goes beyond prescriptions for behavior to develop understandings of problems and issues.

PERRY, CHARLES R., and WILDMAN, WESLEY A. *The Impact of Negotiations in Public Education.* Worthington, Ohio: Jones Publishing Co. 1970. An excellent book based on a comprehensive research project. The material presented is somewhat technical, so a background in understanding basic principles of negotiation would be helpful in understanding the implications of these data.

SARTHORY, JOSEPH A. "Structural Characteristics and the Outcomes of Collective Negotiations." *Educational Administration Quarterly* 7, no. 3 (Autumn 1971): 78–89. This is a report of formal research into the question of the relationship between the composition of bargaining teams and the outcomes of negotiations. These data highlight the importance of care in the selection of a bargaining team.

SCHNAUFER, PETE. *The Uses of Teacher Power.* Chicago: American Federation of Teachers, 1966. This booklet, written by an AFT staff member, reflects a personal point of view. Specific action tactics by which organized teacher groups can bring overt power to bear to force action are analyzed. Consequences of various tactics are discussed.

Selden, David *Winning Collective Bargaining.* Chicago: American Federation of Teachers, 1967. A brief pamphlet with a straightforward, unambiguous presentation of desirable tactics for effective union representation. Mr. Selden, who wrote this while president of the AFT, briefly points directions for locals of his union.

Shils, Edward B., and Whittier, C. Taylor. *Teachers, Administrators, and Collective Bargaining.* New York: Thomas Y. Crowell, 1968. The superintendent of schools and the chief negotiator for the Philadelphia Board of Education at the time of the first formal collective bargaining in that city have collaborated to write a book based largely on their experiences. The book is more than a recapitulation of personal experience. Attention is given to the problems of administration.

Stinnet, T. N.; Kleinmann, Jack; and Ware, Martha L. *Professional Negotiations in Public Education.* New York: Macmillan, 1966. An early book written by authors in leadership positions in the NEA. It is useful as a record of early reactions to a rapidly developing circumstance that entailed problems for the association as well as for employing boards of education.

Tuchman, Barbara. *The Proud Tower.* New York: Macmillan, 1966. This book examines the social, economic, and political circumstances of the Western World just prior to the outbreak of World War I. The forces that led to the creation of modern labor organizations in some nations and of totalitarian governments in others are examined in a very readable manner.

Walton, Richard E., and McKensie, Robert. *A Behavioral Theory of Labor Negotiations.* New York: McGraw-Hill, 1965. A technical analysis of bargaining which develops a scholarly conceptual framework for understanding much typical bargaining activity.

Wolfbein, Seymour L., ed. *Emerging Sectors of Collective Bargaining.* Braintree, Mass.: D. H. Mark Publishing Co., 1970. A number of authorities have contributed chapters to this overview. Both the new directions in bargaining and the nature, conditions, and consequences are treated.

Woodworth, Robert T., and Peterson, Richard B. *Collective Negotiations for Public and Professional Employees.* Glenview, Ill.: Scott, Foresman, 1969. A brief test supplemented by a large number of readings comprises this book. Nearly one-third of the material is directed toward negotiations in public education.

Wortman, Max, and Randle, Wilson C. *Collective Bargaining: Principles and Practices.* Boston: Houghton Mifflin, 1966. This is a basic text providing a scholarly analysis of collective bargaining in industrial relations.